A fresh and exciting approach to some of the m
the human heart.

CW00693623

> —Richard Smoley
> Author, *Inner Christiani*

Authentic Freedom is a revelation toward a new level of spirituality and healing.
This book is rooted in the deepest, yet easy to understand, mysticism. By writing
this masterful piece of work, Lauri Lumby adds herself to a growing number of
advanced healers and authors who understand that since it is the soul that creates
and controls the body, it is only the soul that needs to be healed.

> —Michael Mirdad
> Renowned healer and best-selling author, *The Seven
> Initiations on the Spiritual Path* and *You're Not Going
> Crazy . . . You're Just Waking Up!*

In Authentic Freedom, Lauri Lumby skillfully washes away centuries of dogma to
reveal the powerful and life-changing message at the heart of Christ's teachings
and the universal truths at the core of every religion.

> —Darren Main
> Author of *Yoga and the Path of the Urban Mystic* and *Hearts
> & Minds: Talking to Christians about Homosexuality*

Lauri Lumby takes a refreshing look at the sacred teachings of Jesus, and her words
serve to empower her readers to return to the path of Oneness and Love, to rediscover their connection to the divine. She presents a compelling integration of
the yogic chakra system with the seven deadly sins, and she encourages her readers
to heal themselves and to reestablish themselves in what she coins as "Authentic
Freedom" a life of contentment and joy. Her inclusion of energy healing techniques (such as Reiki) is a welcome challenge to the recently popularized notions
that these energy therapies are incompatible with the underlying messages in Jesus'
teachings. The book will take any reader through a thoughtful process of self-ex-
ploration of Jesus' teachings and of the healing that is possible. It rewrites the path
toward spiritual transformation.

> —Ragani
> Award-winning kirtan recording artist and producer

Lauri Lumby's timely book is radiant, a still point in a currently crazy transitional
world, a well of crystal... reading it has literally given me shivers...it's a home-
coming for me personally, and for all Christians who wondered where the true
undiluted teaching disappeared. A teaching grounded in theology, but totally free
of repressive (and patriarchal) morality. She also writes with a vajra in her hand,
with superb measured clarity . . . *Authentic Freedom* is as fiercely intelligent as it is
uncompromisingly the thing itself.

> —Jay Ramsay
> Author of *Crucible of Love: The Alchemy of Passionate
> Relationships* and *Out of Time: Poem 1998-2008*

Authentic Freedom

Claiming a Life of Contentment and Joy

LAURI ANN LUMBY

St. Johann Press

Haworth, NJ

ST. JOHANN PRESS

Published in the United States of America
by St. Johann Press
P.O. Box 241
Haworth, NJ 07641
www.stjohannpress.com

The paper used in this publication meets the minimum requirements of the American
National Standard for Information Sciences—Permanence of Paper for Printed Library
Materials, ANSI/NISO Z39/48-1992

Interior design and composition by Susan Ramondo (susan@srdesktopservices.com)
Cover design by Gretchen Herrmann, Primary Colors

ISBN 978-1-878282-69-9

Manufactured in the United States of America

CONTENTS

Foreword

I only read or recommend books where I am certain the author has walked her talk.

You are holding such a book.

The moment I met Lauri, to the last page of this book, I witnessed a journey of authenticity that leads my Christian brothers and sisters to personal freedom. This book is a simple and compelling means to claim God's inheritance. Lauri offers genuine ways to heal the separation today's Christians often feel from themselves, God and each other. It is a journey that you take on your own but not alone.

She points the way with a gentle but firm hand encouraging us to heal the divide between us and the Divine. She calls this journey one to *Authentic Freedom*. There are many "freedoms" that present themselves to us that in fact lead us *away* from our true nature and Divine inheritance. To avoid these you need someone who has walked her talk.

Her inquiry practices and exercises guide the reader gently through a process that can only lead to one's true birthrights of inner wisdom and happiness. She doesn't make false promises instead relies on your willingness to heal the divide from your side and take the necessary steps toward your spiritual legacy.

She bravely challenges one's perception of God while borrowing from her studies in Lay Ministry in the Catholic Diocese, reveals Christian practices that offer direct experience with the Divine, and presents real means to the Christian Mystical Experience incorporating the Yogic Chakra system and her studies in Reiki energy. She doesn't hold back and boldly reveals to the reader the hidden teachings of Christ that her studies and practices uncovered.

If you feel a divide within yourself, have had a painful relationship with the church, are searching for means to heal the wounds of the past, or want a journey that uses the teachings of Jesus the Christ, you have found the perfect book. Don't set it down until you know what Lauri knows, God has been within you all along.

Julie Tallard Johnson, MSW, LCSW author
The Wheel of Initiation: Practices for Releasing Your Inner Light.
and director of the Thundering Clouds Retreat Center,
Bear Valley, Wisconsin. www.julietallardjohnson.com

Acknowledgments

To the following I offer a deep prayer of gratitude:

- My parents, Don and Connie Lumby, for their loving support and for the sacrifices they made to send us to parochial schools.

- My maternal grandparents, Wayne and Mildred Evans, for their creative gifts as writers and for inspiring me through their entrepreneurial spirit and commitment to the written and spoken word. I have had a strong sense of their watchful presence in the creation of this book.

- My spiritual teachers and mentors, especially Rev. Jeff VandenHeuvel, Sr. Judy Miller, Leanore Rommelfanger, Sr. Marie Schwaan, Sr. Donna Koch, Sr. Maureen Conroy, Georganne Buyze, and all my teachers and mentors in the Commissioned Ministry and Spiritual Direction Formation programs.

- My writing coach, Julie Tallard Johnson, my local editor Sara Eliasen, and Dave and Diane Biesel of St. Johann Press for your loving guidance, affirmation and support.

- All the students I have had along the way, especially those who participated in the RCIA program which allowed me to discover the most effective format for spiritual formation and to those who have completed the Authentic Freedom process. Thank you for being the ground in which this process could take root and bear fruit.

- My clients who, through their courage to walk their own path and their willingness to invite me to accompany them on that path, allowed the Authentic Freedom concepts to be revealed.

- Aaron and Jason Baer, Rick Maki and Lori Pierquet, current and former owners of the New Moon coffee shop, where much of this book was written. Thanks for the constant flow of caffeine that kept me going through this process.

- My spiritual family in Oshkosh (you know who you are!). I love you.

- Scot Schmidt and our children Maggie and Wil for their loving support through this process and for the sacrifices they have made in helping this dream become real.

- And finally, a deep and prayerful thanks to Jesus, the Christ, my guru, teacher, companion, guide and friend, without whom none of this would be possible and to Mary, the Magdalene who has provided the model of Christian Contemplative witness.

CHAPTER ONE

The Road to Freedom

The Lord God said, "I have witnessed your affliction my people and have heard your cries of complaint against your oppressors, so I know well what you are suffering. Therefore, I have initiated an extraordinary Divine intervention, to rescue you from your oppressors; leading you out of the land of slavery into a good and gracious land, a land flowing with milk and honey."

Exodus 3:7–8 (paraphrased)

Authentic Freedom is a way of life characterized by the consistent experience of inner peace, out of which we are free to openly share the gifts that God has given each of us. Authentic Freedom is our Divine inheritance and the way that God intends us to live! However, instead of claiming this Divine inheritance, most of us struggle through our lives, plagued by the irrational fears, anxieties and compulsions that hold us prisoner. Fortunately, there is a Divinely inspired process—a journey of self-discovery and transformation— that can lead each of us to an awareness of the ways in which fear, false perceptions and illusions block us from realizing the freedom that is authentically ours. That process is Authentic Freedom.

Integration

I would invite you to pause for a few moments of personal reflection. Take a few minutes to reread the passage from Exodus (on page 1). Read it as if it is being addressed directly to you. Then spend some time reflecting on the following questions below, recording your responses in a notebook or journal.

- Where in your life do you feel a profound sense of freedom, peace, love and joy?
- Are you freely and openly sharing the gifts that God has given you?
- Do you feel as if you are able to freely and openly give voice to your truth?
- Where is there fear, constriction, oppression, or restrictions to freedom in your own life?
- What is your own "land of slavery" and what seems to be preventing you from achieving freedom in your life?

Reflecting on these questions, you may have become aware of some areas in your life where you have felt, or perhaps still feel, constricted or even imprisoned. You are not alone; in fact, you are among the majority. By practicing this process of focused reflection, you will learn how to embrace your own authentic freedom and to use the process as a tool that can be returned to again and again in the on-going process of healing.

THE GENESIS OF AUTHENTIC FREEDOM

Authentic Freedom grew out of my own search for peace. I am infinitely grateful for the Divine inspiration that has helped my search evolve from an introduction to the Christian Mystical Prayer Tradition, through an awareness of its connections to the energy flow I witness as a Reiki practitioner, to become the remarkable process for healing that I want to share with you.

To begin with, I don't think my journey is much different than anyone else's. I experienced a normally dysfunctional childhood, graduated from high school, embarked upon the traditional path of college, jobs and relationships. At each juncture and upon the completion of each goal, I believed that I would find happiness and fulfillment. Instead, I found only discontent. No matter which job I held, relationship I entered into, accomplishment I attained, or possession I acquired, a sense of peace eluded me. So, I began to search.

CHRISTIAN MYSTICAL PRAYER

This search, along with some Divine prompting, eventually led me to the Lay Ministry formation program sponsored by my local Catholic Diocese. One class in this program, *Integrative Spirituality*, became the first ingredient in what would eventually become the Authentic Freedom process. In this class, Sr. Marie Schwan, introduced a tradition known as Christian Mystical Prayer. Through this tradition (usually only available to men and women in professed religious life), we were invited to discover and cultivate a deeply intimate and personal relationship with God by embracing a daily practice of mystical prayer through which we would no longer merely know *about* God as defined by some outside perceived authority, but we would come to *know* God directly, through a personal encounter with Divine revelation. I was shocked that after nearly twelve years of Catholic education, I had never been exposed to this approach to prayer. Apparently it had been carefully hidden from my sight all those years.

I immediately embraced a regular practice of mystical prayer and witnessed the profound benefits of maintaining this discipline—reduced stress and anxiety, increased peacefulness and contentment and greater receptivity to insight, creative inspiration and wisdom. After realizing these benefits, I set out to share these techniques with my family and friends. I eventually integrated these practices into the programs I facilitated as a Lay Minister and with my clients in Spiritual Direction. Lectio Divina, Imagination Contemplation, Mantra, Centering Prayer and Contemplative Writing became the foundation from which Authentic Freedom would eventually emerge.

THE REIKI CONNECTION

The second part of this journey came as a result of my training and practice as a Reiki practitioner. Reiki is a form of hands-on healing that came to the West through Dr. Mikao Usui of Japan. Reiki is reminiscent of Jesus' own ministry of healing through its application of touch and prayerful intention of sharing God's healing love for the highest good of the recipient. Reiki works with our body's life force energy—the Divine energy out of which we are made, that flows through our being, giving us life, vitality and health. This energy is recognized in Eastern cultures by many names (Ki, Chi, and Prana, to name a few) and has played an integral role in the Eastern medical traditions for thousands of years. When this energy is balanced and flowing freely, we experience physical, emotional, mental and spiritual wellness. When this energy is blocked or imbalanced, we experience disease. The intention of Reiki is to restore the life force energy to a state of balanced harmony and to release any energy blocks so that the body can return to its natural state of wellness.

Life force energy flows through our body like ocean currents through the sea. This energy can be observed and interacted with using touch, intuition and even sight. In Reiki, as well as in Ayurvedic Medicine and yoga, it is through the chakra system that this life force energy is observed. The chakras are perceived through sense, sight and/or touch as seven wheels of energy located at specific spots along the spinal column and at the crown of the head. (See Appendix B) These wheels of energy correspond to our glandular system and are related to specific organs and their functions. The chakras reflect our physical, emotional, mental and spiritual wellbeing and act as a kind of monitoring system, indicating a state of wellness or disease. The chakras are experienced as open and in a state of equilibrium when we are healthy. When we are in a state of disease, the chakras appear constricted, closed and/or out of balance. Through observation of and interaction with these energy centers, balance can be restored and greater wellness facilitated. Reiki is one healing modality through which this observation, interaction and healing can occur.

A HEALING COMBINATION

After completing the first two levels of Reiki training, I began to offer Reiki as part of my lay ministry work. The response was over-whelmingly positive. Those who received Reiki experienced relief from physical, emotional and mental pain along with a restoration of inner peace and contentment. As I began to incorporate Spiritual Direction into Reiki, the results were even more profound. As I com-bined these practices, I became aware that clients presenting physical complaints often discovered that the root causes resided in unresolved emotional or mental wounds. As the emotional and mental issues were dealt with (either through Spiritual Direction or in combination with traditional therapy) the physical complaints would mysteriously disappear. Over time, I began to observe that there seemed to be a deeper cause for the physical, emotional and mental manifestations of disease. I wondered if the cause might lie in the client's spiritual body.

I brought these questions to prayer, and as I looked at my clients' issues through the perspective of the Christian mystical tradition and through the lens of the chakra correspondences, a pattern emerged. What seemed to be revealing itself was a deeply intimate connection between the physical, emotional and mental correspondences of the chakras and the teachings of Jesus as interpreted through the Christian tradition. As I began to incorporate this theory into my Spiritual Direction and Reiki practices, interesting things began to happen. The woman with chronic pain from fibromyalgia experienced profound relief as she gave herself permission to freely and openly speak her truth. The man with an acute case of acid reflux was freed of his symptoms as he found healthy methods of expressing his anger and resentments. The teenage girl was no longer troubled by unexplainable knee pain as she began to ask for her needs to be met. The food addict was able to overcome this addiction when he confronted his fear that "there was not enough." The divorcee was able to find peace when she realized that she was loved. Each of these individuals experienced healing because they were able to uncover the deeper spiritual wound that was the cause of their physical, emotional and mental pain.

SEVEN CORE FEARS

Using the chakra system as a guide, I attempted to name these deeper spiritual wounds. The end result is what I have come to call the *Seven Core Fears* and they are the root cause of much of our physical, emotional and mental pain. If these spiritual fears are not dealt with, they eventually manifest in our emotions, our minds and our physical bodies. A profound sense of wholeness emerges when we go straight to the spiritual source of the physical, emotional and mental pain and bring healing to these fears. The challenge is that most of the time we are either in denial or are simply unaware that we are struggling with these fears. Authentic

Freedom's process of focused reflection is one of the tools we have to help meet this challenge.

SACRED SEVEN

As I reflected on the *Seven Core Fears*, I realized that we needed a way to more readily recognize these fears. The chakra correspondences provided some help, but a piece seemed to be missing. The notion of "seven" brought me back to my early days in catechism. The Christian tradition is full of references to the number seven—seven days of creation, seven sacraments, seven demons, letters to the seven churches, etc. Could there be a connection between the chakras, the *seven core fears* and the sacred seven of the Christian tradition? I began to explore this possibility and through active study combined with persistent prayer the connection gradually emerged. The *seven core fears* directly corresponded with the Christian tradition of the *seven deadly sins* and the *seven cardinal virtues*. The revelation of this correspondence provided the diagnostic tool (the "sin") as well as the evidence of healing that has taken place (the virtue): the *seven core fears* lead to the *seven deadly compulsions* (sins), the symptoms of which are revealed through the *seven chakras*. Healing these fears allows us to live out the *cardinal virtues*.

The puzzle was nearly complete, but one question remained. What was the path to healing these fears? I found the answer "hidden" in plain sight, in the teachings of Jesus of Nazareth—the Christ.

THE CORE TRUTH AND THE SEVEN SACRED TRUTHS

Hidden within Jesus' teachings and ministry is the *core truth* that Jesus came to reveal—that which Jesus promised as "the truth that shall set you free." It is in living this truth that we experience a life of authentic freedom. Unfortunately, most of us do not know how to access this truth. Instead, we suffer from what I have come to understand as the *core spiritual wound* that is the source of the *seven core fears* and their resulting compulsions.

The good news is that out of his deep love and compassion, Jesus left behind myriad tools to help us heal from this *core wound* and its resulting fears, so that we can enjoy the fullness of life. In fact, Jesus' teachings can all be boiled down to this one *core truth*—that we are one with God, and through that Oneness, one with each other. But, getting to this truth is not always easy. Once the *core fear* has been acknowledged, the resulting compulsion identified and the physical symptom revealed, the *Seven Sacred Truths,* as I have come to call them, provide the path along which realization of the *core truth* can occur, so that ultimately, we can live out the virtues in harmony and peace. When we learn to embrace these *seven sacred truths,* our *core spiritual wound*, along with the resulting spiritual fears, can once and for all be healed and released.

It is this process of healing and transformation that I have come to call the *hidden teachings of Christ.* These teachings will not be found explicitly stated in scripture, nor will they be found in the annals of orthodoxy; rather, they will be revealed through deep contemplation, careful observation and diligent practice, to those who have the eyes to see and the ears to hear. It is for this reason that I call these teachings "hidden." Others have referred to this as the *esoteric* or *mystical* approach. Whatever one calls it, this approach to Jesus' message has been part of the Christian tradition all along, and has grown up right along side the orthodox tradition with which most of us are familiar. Authentic Freedom makes these profound teachings, no longer obscured by orthodoxy, available to everyone.

> *"Gazing with unveiled face, we can now look upon the glory of God and be transformed."*
>
> 2 Corinthians 3:18

Entering into the process of Authentic Freedom, you will discover a powerful tool for healing and transformation. Through scripture, explanation of the Authentic Freedom concepts, and practical exercises in meditation and contemplation (Integration), you will have an opportunity to assimilate new awarenesses into your own life experience. With diligent practice and through the gift of Grace, you will experience the expansive freedom of being released from the fears and compulsions which have held you prisoner within yourself. Freed from these obstacles, you will once again be able to live fully in the peace and joy of who God made you to be. Through this liberation, your own unique giftedness will be able to emerge and you will discover the joy of being able to generously share your gifts in the world. In this way, you shall become a vessel through which God's transforming love and compassion will be released in our world. You will discover for yourself the land of freedom—the good and gracious land, flowing with milk and honey.

In Chart 1 on page 10, you will see at a glance the process of Authentic Freedom. I invite you to take a few moments to focus quietly on each pathway, from left to right, beginning with fear, through the compulsion, to awareness of the chakras, to healing truth and, ultimately, the experience of virtue in your everyday life.

Integration

Before moving on in the journey, I invite you to take some time to reflect on the principles introduced in this chapter. In your own time and in the way the Spirit leads, complete the exercises below.

1. I invite you for just a few minutes to reflect on the seven fears:

   • Where in your life are these fears present, or perhaps glaringly obvious?

Chart 1—Seven Core Fears and Their Pathways to Virtue

Seven Core Fears	Seven Deadly Compulsions	Seven Chakras	Seven Sacred Truths	Seven Cardinal Virtues
There is not enough.	Gluttony	Root	Your Divine Source meets all of your needs in abundance.	Temperance
I will be unable to bring forth life that will persist.	Lust	Sacral	You are co-creator with God and when you surrender to this process, together you bring forth life that persists.	Fortitude
I can't.	Wrath	Solar Plexus	There is nothing outside of you that can keep you from living freely as your most authentic self—the person God made you to be.	Mercy
I am not loved.	Envy	Heart	God is love and you are made of this love. This love cannot be denied, nor does it need to be earned. It is your very being.	Love/Compassion
I am not free to express my truth.	Greed	Throat	Expressing your truth shall set you free!	Generosity
I do not know.	Sloth	Brow	All wisdom, knowledge and truth are available to you through God.	Zeal
I am alone.	Pride	Crown	You are one with God and therefore, never alone.	Humility

- How have these fears stood in the way of your ability to achieve peace and joy in your life?
- Where have these fears stood in the way of your ability to name and claim your own unique giftedness?
- Where have these fears stood in the way of your ability to give full expression to your truth?

In light of these fears, I invite you to take a few minutes to reflect on how these fears may influence your external behaviors:

- Where in your life can you honestly recognize unhealthy compulsions and behaviors that may be rooted in these unhealed fears?
- Where do you feel imprisoned by behaviors that you feel you have no control over? (Addictions are the most obvious, though certainly not the only examples, of these kinds of behaviors—compulsive spending, credit card debt, alcohol and drug addiction are but a few).

2. Take a few minutes to review the *Seven Sacred Truths (see Chart 1).* As you read through these truths, what are your thoughts, your initial reactions? Do you believe that these are true? If your response is, "Yea Right!", then you are exactly where you need to be and this process is definitely for you. 99.9% of us do not recognize these as truth. *Spend some time journaling your thoughts and feelings about these truths. If these are truths you would like to believe, keep reading!*

3. Spend some time with the scripture passage from Exodus on page 12. Read this passage slowly and prayerfully, inviting God to speak to you personally through this passage. Take some time to do some free-form journaling, recording your thoughts and reflection upon reading this passage in this way.

The Lord God said, "I have witnessed your affliction my people and have heard your cries of complaint against your oppressors, so I know well what you are suffering. Therefore, I have initiated an extraordinary Divine intervention, to rescue you from your oppressors; leading you out of the land of slavery into a good and gracious land, a land flowing with milk and honey."

Exodus 3:7–8

CHAPTER TWO

The Core Wound: Healing the Separation

Jesus prayed, "And I have given them the glory you gave me, so that they may be one, as we are one, I in them and you in me, that they may be brought to perfection as one, that the world may know that you sent me, and that you love them even as you loved me."

John 17:22-23

In his human journey, Jesus learned the truth of Oneness with God. It was through the awareness of Oneness that Jesus discovered his true nature as "the Beloved Son of God." It was also through this awareness that Jesus recognized the true nature of all of humanity— that we are each One with God in love, and that through this love, we are One with each other. Jesus' greatest desire, as stated in the prayer above, is that we remember our true nature as One in love with God and with each other. This, then, became Jesus' prayer of healing—healing of the fears and false perceptions that prevent us from remembering the truth of our Oneness. It is this false perception of separation from God that I have come to understand as *the core wound.*

The *core wound* is the source of the longing, restlessness and pain in our human experience. To the extent that this false sense of separation remains, we experience the fears and compulsions that prevent us from living as our most authentic selves; the people God intended us to be; people of peace, of joy and of love, freely and generously sharing the gifts that God has given us. In his book, *The Crucible of Love (pg 215)* Jay Ramsay offers this reflection: "If you can accept that love is our most natural state, then what we find in all of us is an interruption to that state ... It is the core wound in each of us which is our deepest pain and hurt. While it remains closed we are living in the gap—between who we seem to be and who we really are."

Integration

Take a few minutes for personal reflection on the core wound and how you may be experiencing it in your own life. Set aside a few minutes where you can be quiet and still and spend some time reflecting on the following questions. Record this exercise in your journal, if you feel called to do so.

How do you recognize the *core wound* at work in your own life:

- Where do you feel a sense of inner discord?
- Where do you find yourself feeling restless, impatient, frustrated or even angry?
- Do you feel a sense of inner longing, for something that cannot be named?
- Where do you find yourself searching outside of yourself for fulfillment?
- Are you experiencing a life of consistent peace, joy, contentment and freedom?
- Are you openly and freely expressing your unique giftedness in the world?

What has been your own perception of the Presence of the Divine and its proximity within you:

- What are your images of God?
- Do you see God as within you, outside of you, as living in and through you?
- What are the images of God that you were taught as a child and how have they changed or how would you like them to change?

As you reflect upon these questions, you may come in contact with a place of emptiness and longing within yourself. Most of us fall for the illusion that the path to fulfilling this longing exists outside of us, somewhere in the material world. But, if we are truly honest with ourselves, we often observe that despite the acquisition of what we thought would fulfill us, the restlessness and longing soon return— and with a vengeance. The reason for this phenomenon is that the *core wound*, which can never be assuaged by anything "out there," remains unhealed. We have discussed how we can begin to become aware of the *core wound* within us, but where does it come from, what is its purpose and how can we begin to experience its healing?

The origin of this illusion of separation—this *core wound*—is the central mystery of our human experience—a mystery that has yet to be solved, despite the efforts of philosophers, theologians, artists and storytellers throughout recorded history. Why is our human condition such a challenge? Why do we know fear? What is the source of the restlessness and anxiety within us? Unable to comprehend the challenge of the human condition, cultures have created stories to attempt to explain how this challenge came about. In the creation of these tales, the authors have also unwittingly revealed a deeper truth—the recognition of a time when this wound was not part of our experience. A perfect example of this type of storytelling comes from the Judeo-Christian tradition—the story of Adam and Eve.

Most of us are familiar with this tale. Adam and Eve (representatives of the first conscious humans) lived in the Garden of Eden, enjoying a quiet, peaceful, easy existence. All of their needs for food, sustenance and support were met. They freely enjoyed the bounty of the Garden, with one exception. They were NOT to eat of the fruit of the Tree of the Knowledge of Good and Evil. Of course, they were content to obey this command, until the serpent came along. The serpent tempted Adam and Eve; they partook of the fruit and were banished from the Garden, and all of humanity with them. They were cursed to live out the remainder of eternity in struggle and pain. The Hebrews who wrote this lovely myth in an attempt to explain the challenge of the human condition had, in their collective consciousness, a memory of a time of peace and tranquility when no one lived in fear. What changed this peaceful state? Writing from their own unique spiritual lens, they determined that humanity must have angered God and was therefore being punished. This myth comes from a specific cultural perspective that associates favorable happenings with pleasing God and unfavorable happenings with Divine retribution.

Fortunately, this is not the only perspective. Jesus of Nazareth, while sharing the Passover meal with his friends, turned the table on this myth. Throughout all of his ministry, and most specifically in the presence of his disciples, Jesus reveals the truth that brings healing to the *core wound*—to that false sense of separation—shattering the myths and stories that would have us believe otherwise. This is "the truth that shall set us free" (John 8:32). Jesus reveals that we are NOT separate from God, but that in fact, we are One with God, that we always have been and always will be. This is the truth that Jesus (along with other spiritual leaders) came to reveal. This is the truth that threatened the political and religious climate of Jesus' time and while it was for this truth that Jesus was killed, it was also the realization of this truth that allowed Jesus to not only face, but conquer death.

During the Passover meal that Jesus was sharing with his friends, he invoked the following prayer:

> *"Consecrate them in the truth. Your word is truth. I pray not only for them, but also for those who will believe in me through their word, so that they may all be one, as you, Father, are in me and I in you, that they also may be in us, that the world may believe that you sent me. And I have given them the glory you gave me, so that they may be one, as we are one, I in them and you in me, that they may be brought to perfection as one, that the world may know that you sent me, and that you love them even as you loved me."*

John 17:17, 20-23

Through this prayer, Jesus observes the suffering that we experience because of the illusion of separation from God and each other, and asks that we be healed of this *core wound*. He prays that we remember two things:

1. That we are loved by God in the same way that God loves Jesus.
2. That we are One with God through this love.

The truth is, we have not been banished from the Garden. We have not been rejected by God. The source of our pain, Jesus reveals, is the *perception* that we are separate from God. But if it is true, that we are One with God and always have been, why are we still suffering? The reason we remain in this state of longing and restlessness is that we are not yet convinced of God's love for us, or that we are One with God. If this is the central focus of Jesus' message, why do we not believe it and live in the peace and freedom that Jesus promised? The simple answer is that the *core wound* remains unhealed, both within ourselves and within the political, religious, cultural and socioeconomic structures that we construct as a result of our woundedness.

Integration

I now invite you to take a few minutes and reflect on your own experience with the story of Adam and Eve. Reread the Adam and Eve story (Genesis, Chapter 3) prayerfully. Take a few moments to quietly reflect on the following questions recording your thoughts in your journal if you feel so called:

- What is your experience with the Adam and Eve story?
- How has this story colored your perception of God?
- What has your relationship with God been as a result of the idea of human sinfulness and Divine retribution?
- Do you view God as a loving God or a judgmental God whose love you have to earn?
- How would viewing this story as an attempt to explain the core wound open the door to a deeper relationship with God?
- How does the idea of "core wound" free you to embrace the idea of a loving God, rather than a God that has to be placated?

SIN

If we look carefully at the life and teachings of Jesus, we see that he is inviting us to embrace an image of God that is a departure from the traditional image of the Hebrew religious authorities of his time. Jesus was constantly being challenged by the religious authorities who believed in a God whose approval needed to be earned. God's love was thought to be conditional, at best, and only attainable through strict adherence to the law. If you were disobedient to the law, you were known to have lost favor with God and were considered to be a "sinner."

Jesus invited those "who had ears to hear" to consider another possibility. He set forth not only a new image of God, but an entirely new paradigm—a paradigm based on personal relationship and compassion. Having grown in the knowledge of God's love and his Oneness with God, Jesus was able to lead us to his understanding of the truth which sets us free. The God that Jesus knew was a God of unconditional love, compassion and forgiveness. This is the God that Jesus invites us to embrace. When we know God in this way, sin is no longer "that which separates us from God," but merely a symptom of our own false perception of separation. Jesus explains it this way in the noncanonical gospel of Mary Magdalene:

> Peter said to Jesus: "Since you have become the interpreter of the elements and the events of the world, tell us: What is the sin of the world?"
> The Teacher (Jesus) answered, "There is no sin. It is you who make sin exist, when you act according to the habits of your corrupted nature; this is where sin lies."
> Gospel of Mary Magdalene 7:11-19

Sin, when viewed in this way, is no longer subject to judgment, but instead invites us into the greater depths of compassion. "Love the sinner and not the sin," becomes our mantra. When sin is looked upon as a symptom of the fears that come about as a result of an unhealed *core wound*, then all sin becomes an invitation to healing.

From this perspective, we can now look upon even the Jeffrey Daumers and Charles Mansons of our society with compassion. This compassion does not excuse their behavior, but it allows us to see the deeper fears within them that drove them to such heinous acts of violence. In our own journeys, it allows us to let go of the blame, shame and guilt that so often plague our lives. Our compulsive behaviors (sins) are no longer something to look upon in anguish, but something to treat as a wake-up call to a deeper healing being called forth. The compulsive behavior becomes the trigger that alerts us to our false sense of separation, to the need for healing, and invites us to name the fear and allow God to heal us of these fears so that we may once again live in the knowledge that we are loved. In this knowledge of God's love, we know peace, we know joy and we are able to openly and freely share our gifts in the world. It is to this place of Oneness that Jesus invites us when he proclaims, "Repent, for the kingdom of God is at hand." (Matthew 4:17)

Integration

Read and reflect on the following scripture passage and answer the questions below.

> *From that time on, Jesus began to preach and say, "Repent, for the kingdom of God is at hand."*
>
> Matthew 4:17

- What is your understanding of the passage above?
- What does the word "repent" mean to you?
- How do you understand the phrase, "kingdom of God?"

KINGDOM OF GOD

Having been raised in the Catholic Church, the phrase "kingdom of God" meant two things to me. First, it meant heaven—in other words, some place far, far away where I might get to go after I died, but only if I obeyed all the laws, went to Mass on Sundays, said my prayers, gave money to the Church and did good things for others. But even then, I might only get as far as purgatory. "Kingdom of God" also seemed to have something to do with the "Second Coming of Christ," when God would pass final judgment and if we won God's approval, our physical bodies would join us in heaven. That whole concept only confused me, so I chose not to dwell on it. In the end, "Kingdom of God" meant something far away which could only be experienced after we died.

However, Jesus invites us to embrace a deeper understanding.

> *Asked by the Pharisees when the kingdom of God would come, Jesus said in reply, "The coming of the kingdom of God cannot be observed, and no one will announce, 'Look, here it is,' or 'There it is.' For behold, the kingdom of God is within (among) you."*
>
> Luke 17:20-21

> *Jesus said:*
> *"If those who guide you say, 'Look, the Kingdom is in the sky.' Then the birds are closer than you. If they say, 'Look it is in the sea.' Then the fish already know it.*
> *The kingdom is inside you, and it is outside you.*
> *When you know yourself, then you will be known, and you will know that you are the child of the Living God; but if you do not know yourself, you will live in vain."*
>
> Gospel of Thomas Logion 3

The kingdom of God, as explained by Jesus is within us, among us and all around us. Neil Douglas-Klotz, in his groundbreaking work, *Prayers of the Cosmos*, sheds more light on this subject. Jesus, rather than choosing the official temple language of Hebrew to share his message, used the language of the people—Aramaic. According to Douglas-Klotz, the Aramaic language cannot be understood through simple literal translation, since for each word, there are varying depths of meaning and subtle nuances that effect how the word is to be understood. The word kingdom (as in kingdom of God) is translated from the Aramaic word, *malkuthakh*. Literally translated, *malkuthakh* can be taken to mean kingdom, yet being feminine in its form, it would be even better understood to mean "queendom." This idea implies much further discussion for all those religious structures based upon the idea of a masculine God, yet as enticing as that discussion might be, even queendom does not fully express the depth of meaning in the word *malkuthakh*. If we break the word apart into its individual seed sounds and put it back together through the method recommended by Douglas-Klotz, *malkuthakh* means something like this:

> *Malkuthakh (kingdom of God) is the determined extension of the Universal Source of power which draws us toward unity (Oneness) and the visible and experienced sign of that Oneness. It is that which draws us to Oneness and the experience of Oneness itself. In achieving this Oneness, we have reached the fullness of our potential and so has God.*

A far cry from the images of heaven as far, far away, only to be experienced after death, ruled by an old-man king, sitting on a golden throne surrounded by the heavenly host, wouldn't you say? *Malkuthakh* invites us to be open to the movement of the Divine Source that is both within us and outside of us. This movement draws us closer and closer into that place of complete Oneness with this Source and with all of creation. As we are drawn toward this Oneness, we are able to experience the hallmarks of Oneness in our lived existence. As we come to know the truth of God, we come to know our own truth more fully and as we come to know ourselves, we come to know God. Entering into this process, we move toward the fullness of our human potential. This is the Good News that Jesus came to reveal, that the Kingdom of God is NOW and that it is here in our very midst!

Integration

I invite you to pause for a few minutes of personal reflection. Record your responses in your journal if you feel so called. Prayerfully reread the two scripture passages below related to the kingdom of God. Reflect on these passages then answer the reflection questions that follow.

Asked by the Pharisees when the kingdom of God would come, Jesus said in reply, "The coming of the kingdom of God cannot be observed, and no one will announce, 'Look, here it is,' or 'There it is.' For behold, the kingdom of God is within (among) you."

Luke 17:20-21

Jesus said:
"If those who guide you say, 'Look, the Kingdom is in the sky.' Then the birds are closer than you. If they say, 'Look it is in the sea.' Then the fish already know it.

The kingdom is inside you, and it is outside you.

When you know yourself, then you will be known, and you will know that you are the child of the Living God; but if you do not know yourself, you will live in vain."

Gospel of Thomas Saying 3

If the Kingdom of God is known by experiences of peace, love and joy, take some time to recall moments in your own life where you have had these experiences:

- How have you experienced or known peace?
- When have you known love?
- When have you experienced joy?
- What are your thoughts about the Kingdom of God as being present in the here and now?
- How does this challenge your formerly held beliefs?

REPENTENCE

If what we are saying is true, that the Kingdom of God is present here and now, how do we find it? Jesus offers us a practical formula for cultivating awareness of the kingdom. In a word, the formula is to repent. ("Repent, for the kingdom of God is at hand.") The word *repent* is most often understood to mean confessing remorse for your sins and promising to give them up. However, based on what we have already explored regarding the nature of our compulsive behaviors, a deeper understanding is required. If our "sins" are symptoms of the fear within us that springs from an unhealed *core wound*, then confessing them and promising to refrain from these behaviors is simply not enough.

Repent means more than confessing our sins and promising to give them up. If we look again to Neil Douglas-Klotz and his spiritual study of the Aramaic Jesus, we discover that repentance has a much deeper meaning.

> *"Repent can also mean to return, come again, flow back, or ebb. Its roots show something that turns or returns, as though in a circle or spiral, to its origin or its original rhythm. In a Hebrew-Aramaic sense, to repent means to unite with something by affinity, because it feels like going home."*
>
> (Douglas—Klotz, Neil; *The Hidden Gospel* pg 85)

When we look at repentance in this way, we can begin to see that this is the foremost desire of our human journey—to return to our Source. It is in returning again and again to our Source in present-moment awareness, in prayer and meditation, in care of the self and gratitude for our world, that we shall come to know the kingdom of God. In returning again and again to God who is the source of all healing, we are freed of the fears that cause the compulsive behaviors which drive us to look outside ourselves for fulfillment and peace, and are empowered to more fully embrace a life of authentic freedom—ultimately, another phrase for "kingdom of God."

The cause and purpose of our human existence is to repent so that we can grasp the good news that the kingdom of God is HERE and NOW! As we come to know more fully the Source that made us, we begin to discover the truth of who we are. Knowing that we are loved and that through this love we are One with God, we are able to experience the peace and contentment that is God's intention for us. As we come to know this truth we can, through our own unique giftedness, become vehicles through which this truth can be revealed in our world, fulfilling God's desire to manifest heaven on earth. Authentic Freedom gives you the tools through which you will be empowered to participate in this act of co-creation, enabling you to not only know, but to be part of the revelation of the Kingdom of God—right here, right now!

AUTHENTIC FREEDOM—AN INITIATORY PATH

Jesus discovered his Oneness with God and knew that we, too, share in this Divine inheritance. Jesus was also well aware that he was loved by God and that there was nothing that could separate him from that love. This is Jesus' revelation for us. This is the truth that Jesus promised would set us free. The purpose of Jesus' life on earth was to share this good news with as many people as would listen, to bring healing to those who still suffered from the *core wound* that is a false sense of separation and to give us the tools to continue this process in our own lives. Jesus knew that when we overcome this *core wound*, we will know the peace that God intended for us and that in this place of harmony, we will no longer be plagued by the fears and compulsions that arise out of this perception of separation. It is in this way that Jesus came to "save us from our sins." This is what Jesus meant when he said to those he healed, "Your sins are forgiven." Jesus was not an allopathic physician, treating merely symptoms. He knew that the outward behaviors and physical manifestations were simply reflective of an unhealed *core wound*. He healed people holistically, at their very core—helping them to embrace the truth of Oneness in God's love so that they would be free of the fears and compulsions that plagued their lives. In this way, his healing was and is truly complete.

Mary Magdalene is one example of the completeness of Jesus' healing and the healing that is possible for us. Thanks to modern scripture scholarship, Mary Magdalene has been rescued from her formerly maligned role as "adulterous woman." We now know more fully the truth of Mary's role as a close disciple of Jesus, participant in his ministry and first witness to the resurrection. Commissioned by Christ to deliver the message of the resurrection to the other disciples, Mary has been aptly titled *Apostle to the Apostles.*

What has always been held as true of her is that through Jesus' healing, she was released of seven demons. Traditionally, this would represent demonic possession, or at best, serious mental illness. Fortunately, modern exploration of Gnostic writings and philosophies offers another possibility. Jean Yves-Leloup in his translation and commentaries on the Gospel of Mary Magdalene, the Gospel of Philip, and the Gospel of Thomas theorizes that being cured of seven demons represented an initiatory path. Mary Magdalene, he contends, was successful in completing a formal program of initiation facilitated by Jesus. Through this process, she was released of the fears and compulsions that prevented her from remembering her Oneness with God, and upon the completion of her initiation, she was able to embrace this Oneness and to embody God's love. She was made whole. It was only in completing this initiatory path that she was able to receive the message of the resurrection and deliver the good news to the apostles. Through Jesus' compassionate and loving presence, Mary was freed of the demons (fears) that kept her from living as the whole and unified person that God had intended. In this place of wholeness, she knew peace, love, joy and contentment and was able to freely share her gifts in the world.

> The disciples asked him, "Shall we become as infants to enter into the Kingdom?"
>
> Yeshua answered them, "When you make the two into One, when you make the inner like the outer and the high like the low; when you make male and female into a single One . . . then you will enter into the Kingdom."
>
> Gospel of Thomas Saying 22

Although we no longer have the formal program of initiation through which Mary Magdalene was led, we do have the teachings of Jesus and we have the gift of his Holy Spirit. Authentic Freedom rescues scripture from doctrinal interpretation and places it directly into your hands where it will become the living, breathing word of God. The next seven chapters will provide you with the opportunity and the tools to contemplate sacred scripture along with ancient traditions of Christian mysticism so that, like Mary Magdalene, you can embark upon your own path of initiation, acknowledging any of the *seven core fears* or *compulsions* that may be blocking you from experiencing Oneness with God, and transforming these fears into the healing truth that will make you whole and set you free.

CHAPTER THREE

Abundance Is Yours

Therefore I tell you, do not worry about your life, what you will eat (or drink), or about your body, what you will wear. Is not life more than food and the body more than clothing? Look at the birds in the sky; they do not sow or reap, they gather nothing into barns, yet our Creator feeds them. Are not you more important than they?

Matthew 6:25-26

*A*bundance is the buzz word in our popular culture today. Hundreds of books and now even movies have been produced to tell us that God loves us so much that we deserve to have everything we want; that all we have to do is think the right thoughts and we can create our dream reality; that the law of attraction guarantees that we will have what we think about (good or bad). And, if we do not have what we want, it is our fault because we are resonating with the wrong feelings, thoughts and emotions.

All of these philosophies are based on two grave misconceptions:

1. Abundance is measured by acquisition of what we want.
2. Acquisition of what we want will give us happiness and peace.

In our Western, consumeristic culture, abundance has been defined as "stuff." The more stuff we have, the more abundant we are. As such, abundance is recognized by the right cars, the biggest house, the most elaborate vacations and membership in the most prestigious clubs. Hollywood and the popular media capitalize on this cultural phenomenon as they continually bombard us with images and stories of the "Rich and Famous." There is nothing wrong with a "rich and famous" lifestyle, and there are many who are rich and famous who truly know peace. But the question must be asked, is it the *stuff* that is the true source of their peace? Would getting more stuff give us the fulfillment we so desperately desire? Does acquiring the wealth we covet give us a sense of abundance in the truest sense? Based on the level of discontent we see in our society, in spite of the material prosperity enjoyed by many, I sense that the answer is no. The hard truth is that stuff will never be the remedy to the first core fear—*the fear that there is not enough.*

THE FEAR—THERE IS NOT ENOUGH

In understanding the fear that *there is not enough,* we must first distinguish between the instinctive, biological fears that help us to survive and the illogical, irrational fears that keep us from living fully. Our human body is programmed to respond in fear to anything that it perceives to be life-threatening. This response is helpful when the threat is real, as when we are faced with starvation, or in physical danger for example. However, this response is not helpful when the threat is only imagined. In these situations, the reptilian brain cannot distinguish between actual threat and perceived threat. (See more on this subject see *The Instinct to Heal* by David Servan—Schreiber and *Waking the Tiger* by Peter Levine.)

Obviously we need food, clothing and shelter to live. When these needs are not being met, the fear that *there is not enough* is valid. On the other hand, when we have the food, clothing and shelter we need to survive, this fear becomes a distortion. It is this distortion that we will address through the Authentic Freedom process.

It is all too easy to observe this fear in the constant mantras of our modern world: not enough food, not enough shelter (or not enough of the right houses, in the right neighborhoods), not enough of the right clothes, not enough of the right jobs, positions of status or power, not enough money, money, money, books, toys, friends, lovers, people to admire us, things to collect, activities to keep us occupied, and finally, time in which to do it all and have it all. Our lives have become a compulsive quest to get the money necessary to acquire more and better stuff so that we can be admired as people of position, status and power, and we are plagued by the fear that there won't be time to get it all done. No wonder our lives are mountains of stress.

In the end, the fear that *there is not enough* blocks our ability to trust in God. In this constant striving to satisfy the fear that there is not enough, we have forgotten Jesus' words of comfort and his invitation to recognize that it is not the stuff that is the ultimate source of fulfillment.

> *Therefore I tell you, do not worry about your life, what you will eat (or drink), or about your body, what you will wear. Is not life more than food and the body more than clothing? Look at the birds in the sky; they do not sow or reap, they gather nothing into barns, yet our Creator feeds them. Are not you more important than they?*
>
> Matthew 6:25-26

In this reading, Jesus reminds us that the source of life is not in things outside of ourselves. He knows that we need food and shelter to survive, but he is reminding us that there is a source through which we can find release from the worries and fears that plague us. This Source, he reminds us, is God. When we stand in the place of fearing that *there is not enough*, we can turn to God for healing and release from these fears. Even if we are in the seemingly desperate position of staring death in the face, our connection with God can give us peace. Even the lack of adequate food, shelter and protection cannot separate us from the peace of God. In the end, we are invited to understand that abundance is an inner experience independent of the external circumstances of our lives.

Integration

I invite you to take a few minutes to reflect on the fear *There is not enough* and how you may be experiencing it in your own life.

- Do you find yourself anxious about money, things, time?
- Where do you find yourself acquiring things you do not really need?
- Open your closet and your drawers, look on your shelves; how many of those items remain unused or unworn?
- What if you were asked to give away all of your belongings, which ones would you have the greatest difficulty releasing and why?

DEADLY COMPULSION—GLUTTONY

The fear that *there is not enough* creates within us a deep emptiness that we are then provoked to fill. The drive to satisfy this emptiness appears in our life experience as the compulsion known as *gluttony*. *Gluttony*, as we shall discover, forever seeks but is never fulfilled. Merriam-Webster defines gluttony as "excess in eating or drinking." Although this is one way to understand *gluttony*, when we look at it from a spiritual perspective, a broader meaning is revealed. When surrounded by the fear of lack that comes from having forgotten our Oneness with God, we search outside of ourselves for fulfillment. This compulsion to seek outside ourselves for the remedy to our inner emptiness is lived out as *gluttony* and drives us to a deep attachment to our material possessions, wealth, status and power. Jesus reminds us that the things outside of us do not provide fulfillment, but that fulfillment is realized only in a deep connection with our Divine Source—that which we call God.

Integration

Let us take a few minutes for personal reflection. Spend a few minutes praying with the scripture passage below. Then answer the reflection questions that follow:

> Jesus said, "Do not store up for yourselves treasures on earth, where moth and decay destroy, and thieves break in and steal. But store up treasures in heaven, where neither moth nor decay destroys, nor thieves break in and steal. For where your treasure is, there also will your heart be."
>
> Matthew 6:19-21

Take a few minutes to reflect on the spiritual understanding of gluttony:

- What are your thoughts and reflections about this new understanding?
- Where might you be experiencing *gluttony* in your own life?
- What is the cause of *gluttony* in your own life and how might you invite God to heal you from this compulsion?

- What are your treasures and where are you storing them up—are they outside or inside yourself?
- Where is your heart, in your material possessions or in your connection with God?
- How would you like to see this transformed?

How do we recognize the compulsion of *gluttony* as active in our lives? Remember that *gluttony*, from a spiritual perspective, is any action that comes out of the false belief that something outside of us, something other than God, will be our source of fulfillment. The most obvious form of *gluttony* from this perspective is the acquisition or desire of material objects in the hopes that they will fill the empty space inside. But, *gluttony* shows up in many other ways. We are familiar with *gluttony* in its traditional form as overeating. Overconsumption of any kind is gluttony. Anytime we consume more than we really need to survive, we are being gluttonous—including the situations in which we ravage our natural resources so as to create shortage or lack. Our Divine Source has given us all the natural resources we need as a planet to survive. In this day of modern convenience, it is only through overconsumption and unjust distribution of resources that we have created lack.

Beyond material goods and resources, *gluttony* is also known in our compulsive-addictive behaviors. Consumerism, racism, sexism, bigotry and discrimination are all forms of gluttony. Addictions to alcohol, drugs, sex and gambling are all forms of *gluttony*. Individuals practicing these addictions continually reach outside of themselves through substances and behaviors for something that will dull their inner agony, believing the substances to be relief from the pain.

It is easy to understand *gluttony* when it comes to behaviors of overconsumption and addiction. It is more difficult to understand this compulsion from the other end of the spectrum in which it is also engaged: deprivation. Deprivation is the mirror image of overconsumption. When we deprive ourselves of the things that we need to survive, we too are engaging in the compulsion of *gluttony*. Anorexia Nervosa (when seen as an addiction to deprivation) is an example of this form of *gluttony*. Someone with this compulsion is literally starving herself to death—a clear form of *gluttony* from this perspective of deprivation.

Beyond our basic survival needs, we are also engaging in the compulsion of *gluttony* when we deprive ourselves of those things that are life-enriching. We have a basic human right to survive and the right to have our needs met, and that encompasses those needs beyond mere survival—the needs that make life worth living, such as time to play; to be with God; to nurture and cultivate joy, peace and love; to forge healthy intimate relationships; to perform work that is fulfilling; and, to indulge our creative gifts. If we deprive ourselves of the things that make life worth living, we are again engaging the compulsion of *gluttony*.

Integration

Prayerfully read the scripture passage that follows and answer the reflection questions.

> Then Jesus told them a parable. "There was a rich man whose land produced a bountiful harvest. He asked himself, 'What shall I do, for I do not have space to store my harvest?' And he said, 'This is what I shall do: I shall tear down my barns and build larger ones. There I shall store all my grain and other goods, and I shall say to myself, "Now as for you, you have many good things stored up for many years, rest, eat, drink, be merry!"' But God said to him, 'You fool, this night your life will be demanded of you; and the things you have prepared to

whom will they belong?' Thus will it be for one who stores up treasure for himself but is not rich in what matters to God."

Luke 12:16-21

- What behaviors are you engaging in that could be considered gluttonous? Where are you storing up, collecting, acquiring more than you actually need?
- Where are your patterns of over-consumption?
- Where are your patterns of self-deprivation?
- Where are you not making sure that your needs are being met in regards to life-giving activities that nurture your soul and the creative gifts that God has given you?
- Where do you feel you are not deserving of having your needs met?

As Jesus teaches us, riches, in and of themselves, are not bad; it is our attachment to them that indicates that perhaps we have used them as a replacement for God, hoping that in acquiring these goods we might finally find peace. God alone is the source of peace, and this is the truth that Jesus reminds us to embrace. Very few, if any of us, are truly free of this wound. We all struggle with this fear that *there is not enough* and its prevalence in our lives. The tricky thing is that most of the time we are ignorant of this fear and the effects it is having on us physically, mentally, emotionally and spiritually. This is where knowledge of the *Chakra System* can be very helpful.

EASTERN MEDICINE AS A TOOL FOR HEALING— THE ROOT CHAKRA

As mentioned earlier, each chakra corresponds to a specific core fear. The fear that *there is not enough* is related to the *root chakra*—

located at the base of the spine. The *root chakra* governs and reflects our connection with the earth and all the resources it provides for our physical survival. If we live in fear that *there is not enough*, the energy of the *root chakra* shifts into a state of imbalance. Biologically, the *root chakra* governs our lower extremities—those parts of the body most connected with earth. Also, the *root chakra* governs our processes of elimination as it is through this biological process that we give back to the earth what the earth gave to us so that it can be recycled and renewed. On a physical level, the *root chakra* governs and reflects the state of health of our colon, our large intestines, the adrenal glands and kidneys, the lower back, buttocks, legs, knees and feet. When we suffer unexplained disease or weakness in any of the aforementioned body parts, it may be an indication that the *root chakra* is unbalanced.

However, when our *root chakra* is in a state of health, we are open to receiving all that we need and we take only what we need to survive. Spiritually, the *root chakra* reflects our ability to exist on this earthly plane in a state of contentment and trust. We are fully present to our physical bodies and realize that we are a spiritual being living a physical existence. All of the physical manifestations of Spirit are embraced as good. We are connected with the earth and feel safe and secure in our environment. Emotionally the *root chakra* in a state of health allows us to feel safe, secure and at peace. Mentally, we are free from worry and move through our lives with ease, able to accomplish our dreams effortlessly. Physically, we are strong, robust and thriving. We feel at one in our physical bodies.

One day as Jesus was teaching, Pharisees and teachers of the law were sitting there who had come from every village of Galilee and Judea and Jerusalem, and the power of the Lord was with him for healing. And some men brought on a stretcher a man who was paralyzed; they were trying to bring him in and set him in his presence. But not finding a way to bring him in because of the crowd, they went up on the roof and lowered him on the stretcher through the tiles into the middle in front of Jesus. When he saw their faith he said, "As for you, your sins are forgiven." Then the scribes and Pharisees began to ask themselves, "Who is this who speaks blasphemies? Who but God alone can forgive sins?" Jesus knew their thoughts and said to them in reply, "What are you thinking in your hearts? Which is easier to say, 'Yours sins are forgiven,' or to say, 'Rise and walk?' But that you may know that the Son of Man has authority on earth to forgive sins"—he said to the man who was paralyzed, "I say to you, rise, pick up your mat, and go home." He stood up immediately before them, picked up what he had been lying on, and went home, glorifying God.

Luke 5:17-25

Integration

I invite you at this time to learn and put into practice a prayer form with which you may not yet be familiar. The prayer form, popularized by St. Ignatius of Loyola, invites us to pray through our daydreaming. Through *Imagination/Contemplation* we allow God to speak to us through our creative imagination, typically using narrative scripture stories as the starting block. I invite you to prayerfully read through the previous scripture passage. As you are reading, choose a character that you might resonate with—the paralytic man, his friends, Jesus, the scribes or Pharisees or even an unnamed bystander. Imagine yourself to be that person, witnessing the event as it unfolds. Immerse yourself in the story, imagining the scenery, what you are wearing, the weather, the smells, etc.

Allow the story to unfold in your mind as if you are participating in the story. Allow your imagination to run wild. After you have allowed the story to unfold, record in your journal what you saw and in particular, what you were feeling as the events unfolded.

After writing, go back and read your journal entry, and spend some time reflecting on what emerged and how that may be related to your own journey. Record these reflections in your journal as well. What did God reveal to you through this exercise?

So far, our journey to Authentic Freedom has introduced us to our *core wound*, the false perception of separation from God, and this *core wound* has led us to discover the first manifestation of this wound in the fear that *there is not enough*. This fear is then demonstrated through a set of compulsions and behaviors (such as overconsumption and deprivation) known as *gluttony*, which screams for attention by perpetuating an imbalance in the *root chakra* and all the organs to which its energy flows. We are now ready for the next step in the Authentic Freedom process. We will now explore the healing truth that removes the power from the fear of *not enough*, and helps us to remember more fully our original nature as peaceful, loving, joyful beings—the *sacred truth* of *abundance* and the knowledge that it is our Divine Source that meets all of our needs.

Integration

I invite you at this time to pause for a few minutes of personal reflection. Take some time to reflect on the following questions related to abundance, recording your thoughts in your journal.

- What is your current understanding of the word abundance?
- How have you experienced abundance in your own life?
- Have you found that the acquisition of material goods has given you the peace and contentment that you seek?
- Where have you witnessed people who seem to possess a deep inner peace?

- Was material acquisition a source of their peace, in your opinion?

SACRED TRUTH—YOUR DIVINE SOURCE MEETS ALL OF YOUR NEEDS IN ABUNDANCE

Abundance, as a spiritual quality is independent of the external circumstances of our lives. Spiritual *abundance* is known by a deep experience of inner peace and contentment. The following story from Mark's gospel illustrates this understanding of *abundance*.

> *As Jesus was setting out on a journey, a man ran up, knelt down before him, and asked him, "Good teacher, what must I do to inherit eternal life?" Jesus answered him, "Why do you call me good? No one is good but God alone. You know the commandments: 'You shall not kill; you shall not commit adultery; you shall not steal; you shall not bear false witness; you shall not defraud; honor your father and your mother.'" He replied and said to him, "Teacher, all of these I have observed since my youth." Jesus, looked at him, loved him and said to him, "You are lacking one thing. Go, sell what you have, and give to the poor and you will have treasure in heaven; then come, follow me." At that statement his face fell, and he went away sad, for he had many possessions.*
>
> *Jesus looked around and said to his disciples, "How hard it is for those who have wealth to enter the kingdom of God!" The disciples were amazed at his words. So Jesus again said to them in reply, "Children, how hard it is to enter the kingdom of God! It is easier for a camel to pass through the eye of a needle than for one who is rich to enter the kingdom of God." They were exceedingly astonished and said among themselves, "Then who can be saved?"*

Mark 10:17–26

Integration

I invite you to pause for a few moments to bring the previous reading into your own personal prayer. Because this reading has often been interpreted from the perspective of a judgmental, punitive God, I would invite you to take a few moments of preparation. First, invite God to heal you of any lingering thoughts of a punitive God so that you may read this instead from the perspective of compassion. Read through this passage prayerfully, inviting Christ to reveal to you the deeper meaning of this passage. Record your reflections in your journal if you feel so called.

There is much to be observed in this short interchange between Jesus, the rich man and Jesus' disciples. Reading this passage with the idea of *abundance* in mind, several items stand out. Twice in this reading, the author of this gospel refers to the disciples as being "amazed" and "astonished." What in this reading created such a dramatic reaction? At this point, we can assume that the disciples knew Jesus reasonably well, so what was it that amazed them in this teaching? It is important when reflecting on this passage to remember that the Hebrew theology at the time of Jesus held that if you were rich, it was because you had found favor with God. The rich man in this passage would have been assumed to be guaranteed a place in the kingdom of God as he was already in God's good graces as reflected by his material wealth. Instead, Jesus turns the table on this long-held belief. Not only was the rich man not guaranteed the kingdom of heaven, it would be harder for him to enter than it would be for a camel to pass through a needle's eye. Even more surprising is that the man insisted that he had upheld Mosaic Law since the time of his youth. Along with riches, status and power, Mosaic Law was the other ticket to heaven in the eyes of the Hebrew people. If one had upheld the law, it was certain that they would enjoy eternal life. Jesus implies that even the law is not enough. No wonder the disciples were astonished.

How is it that the rich man cannot enter the kingdom of heaven when he possesses the rewards for a life well lived? How is it that the law is not enough? How can Jesus ask the man to get rid of the very gift that God has presumably granted him for being a just and righteous person? It seems instead that Jesus is punishing the man for having wealth by denying him the kingdom of God. How is this reading to be understood? Taken from the viewpoint of a punitive, judgmental God, wealth becomes a pawn in the quest for eternal reward. If we change our perspective and look at this with compassion, a contrasting meaning begins to emerge. Recall for a moment what Jesus means when he referred to the "kingdom of God". Contrary to the common Western interpretation of this phrase, "kingdom of God" does not refer to some heavenly dwelling far, far, away, only to be enjoyed by the few chosen ones after their earthly life. Jesus is constantly inviting his followers to recognize and enjoy the kingdom of God in the here and now. Jesus is aware of all the things in our human experience that stand in the way of our ability to enjoy the peace, love and joy that are the hallmarks of the kingdom. Recognizing the *core wound* as the false perception of separation from God, Jesus sets about healing people of the fears and compulsions that stand in the way of their ability to believe in the truth of Oneness. In the case of the rich man, *"Jesus looked at him, loved him and said to him, 'You are lacking one thing. Go, sell what you have, and give to the poor and you will have treasure in heaven; then come, follow me.'"* In looking on the rich man with love, Jesus saw into his soul and recognized that the stumbling block to his peace and contentment was not the riches themselves, but his attachment to material wealth. Jesus was not judging the wealth as bad, but simply recognizing that the rich man had an attachment to his wealth that was standing in the way of his spiritual freedom. The rich man's response confirms what Jesus saw: *"At that statement his face fell, and he went away sad, for he had many possessions."* Unable to conceive of the idea of letting go of his riches, the rich man is now further burdened by the sadness of knowing it is this attachment that keeps him from knowing peace.

Abundance as represented in this reading is measured by our reliance on God, not by material wealth. Jesus goes on to explain:

> *"Amen, amen, I say to you there is no one who has given up house or brothers or sisters or mother or father or children or lands for my sake and for the sake of the gospel who will not receive a hundred times more now in this present age; houses and brothers and sisters and mothers and children and lands, with persecutions and eternal life in the age to come. The many that are first will be last and the last will be first."*
>
> Mark 10:29-31

What Jesus is saying is that it is in giving up our attachments that we are free to dwell in the place of Oneness with God. In other words, if we believe that our material possessions, our land, our status, or achievements, or our loved ones are the source of fulfillment, then we, like the rich man, will go away empty. On the other hand, if we recognize that the true source of fulfillment is in God, then there shall be our reward.

HOLY VIRTUE—TEMPERANCE

By integrating the truth of *abundance* you will realize healing and release of the fear that *there is not enough* and become empowered to rest in the contentment of knowing that your Divine Source is lovingly and generously providing for all of your needs. Resting in the grace of contentment, your experience will begin to reflect the holy virtue of *temperance*. No longer restless in the insecurity of worry, you will become grateful for what you have and willing to generously share your abundance. By allowing this fear to be healed, you will move more and more deeply into the truth of Oneness with God and will experience more fully the promise of God's freedom. I leave you with the following scripture passages as a foundation of the work you are accomplishing and as preparation for the next step in this journey—healing of the fear that *you will not be able to bring forth life that will persist.*

> *But seek first the kingdom of God and his righteousness and all these things will be given to you besides.*
>
> Matthew 6:33

> *Ask and it will be given to you; seek and you will find; knock and the door will be open to you. For everyone who asks, receives; and the one who seeks finds; and to the one who knocks, the door will be opened.*
>
> Matthew 7:7-8

CHAPTER FOUR

You Are Uniquely Gifted

Jesus said, "This is how it is with the kingdom of God; it is as if a man were to scatter seed on the land and sleep and rise night and day and the seed would sprout and grow, he knows not how. Of its own accord the land yields fruit, first the blade, then the ear, then the full grain in the ear. And when the grain is ripe, he wields the sickle at once, for the harvest has come."

Mark 4:26-29

Who are you—REALLY??? Are you your job, your family, your education, your status, your power? Is the person you present to the world really you, or is there a deeper truth within? If you are like most human beings, the highest truth of who you are is locked up deep within your being, like an acorn seed that hides within it the magnificent oak. What is the magnificence within *you* that is waiting to be revealed?

CORE FEAR—I CANNOT BRING FORTH LIFE THAT WILL PERSIST

Perhaps this question has you stumped. After all, how many of us truly believe in our own magnificence? Not many. And, sadly, even for those who do, there is the whole matter of what to do about it, given the fact that we have to earn a living, raise the kids, clean the house . . . Our own magnificence is usually not much of a priority! I suspect most of us are actually somewhat afraid of what we could do if we felt magnificent, and so we lead our "lives of quiet desperation" with the vague fear that we will do nothing , become nothing, and leave nothing behind because we do not know how or are unable to bring forth life (physically or as creative expression) that will persist.

This fear, that *we are unable to bring forth life that persists*, is the second core fear that dictates much of our experience of brokenness—broken trust, broken dreams, broken relationships, broken hearts, a broken world. Faced with this brokenness, we are compelled to ask, if God has planted a seed of magnificence within each of us, and if we have no choice but to become who God intended us to become, then why have the peace and love of God not yet been fully realized within us and within our world? The answer, of course, is fear. When we have forgotten the *core truth* that we are One with God and with each other, we are unable to enter fully into the process that allows our true selves to emerge. We are like the acorn that, instead of finding its way to fertile soil is stomped on and crushed, unable to bring forth the magnificent oak within.

> *Jesus spoke in this parable: "A sower went out to sow his seed. And as he sowed, some seed fell on the path and was trampled, and the birds of the sky ate it up. Some seed fell on rocky ground, and when it grew, it withered for lack of moisture. Some seed fell among thorns, and the thorns grew with it and choked it. And some seed fell on good soil, and when it grew, it produced fruit a hundredfold."*
>
> Luke 8:5-8

The temptation in this reading is to look at it from the perspective of the victim. We are quick to blame our external circumstances for our inability to fully realize and make manifest our own unique giftedness. We have forgotten that the peace and love of God are not dependent upon our external circumstances. As Jesus continually reminds us, the kingdom of God is an internal experience. As such, the ability of our true self to emerge is not in any way related to what is happening outside of us. Even in the direst of human circumstances, God's magnificence will continue to be revealed. We need only be open to perceiving it. With that in mind, we are invited to reflect on the Parable of the Sower from a new perspective.

Integration

Read the parable of the sower (page 46) slowly and reflectively, then answer the reflection questions below.

- Where have you planted your seed?
- Have you scattered it about to be trampled and eaten?
- Have you carelessly placed it in rocky ground, then neglected to water it?
- Have you scattered it among thorns?
- Have you placed it in fertile soil then carefully tended it?

The energy of God within us that compels us to become our most authentic selves is the energy of procreation. Through this dynamic, God is experiencing God's self over and over, in infinite ways. It is through the process of physical procreation that we can best understand the fear *I will not be able to bring forth life that will persist.* We know from a biological perspective that one of greatest survival instincts is continuation of the species. As such, we are hardwired to seek opportunities through which the human race can continue to exist. This instinctual drive cannot be contained. For us to continue to live and thrive on this earth, we must find a partner with whom we can bring forth more of our own. The inner restlessness that compels us to seek out this partner is very closely related to fear in that failure to connect with this partner means we will not be able to play our part in contributing to the on-going survival of our species.

This inner restlessness is the same energy that churns within us when God is seeking to find expression through us through our own unique giftedness. The unique person that God created us to be and through which God desires to find expression cannot be born without our willing participation. Saying yes to the procreative energy of God within allows our true selves to emerge, helping to bring us to the place of peace and joy that is our true nature. The challenge is that to fully embrace the person God intends us to be, we have to let go of much of what we think we know about ourselves. Like the acorn, we have to shed our outer shell, which is constructed of our fears, false perceptions and ego attachments, so that the true self is able to emerge. To our fearful ego, shedding this outer shell is akin to death. To embrace our true selves, our false self must die, and it is this death that we fear in the process of self-actualization. We cling to the life that we have known, afraid to embrace the potential of a life not-yet lived. This fear then becomes a paradox: we are afraid that *we are unable to bring forth life* (our own magnificence) *that will persist* while fearing the death we are sure to face in bringing forth this new life. No wonder few of us ever reach the fullness of our human potential. We are both afraid of living, and afraid of dying. It is this paradoxical fear that God desires to heal within us.

When we get stuck in this paradox, most of us prefer to err on the side of safety; we don't want to take the risk of dying to our old self to give life to the unique gifts residing in our souls. In denying the unique way in which we are gifted to reveal God in the world, we are indulging the compulsion of *lust*.

DEADLY COMPULSION—LUST

Before we can understand *lust* as a spiritual compulsion, we have to remove it from its usual association with sexual desire. The nature of sexual desire is mostly a mystery, but seems to be primarily a biochemical response related to our instinctive drive to continue the species. A healthy sexual relationship is based on mutual honor, respect and participation in which both partner's needs are honored as sacred and equal effort is given toward the fulfillment of those needs. Mutuality is what distinguishes normal, healthy, sexual desire from *lust. Lust* has nothing to do with mutuality. *Lust* is about power and control.

While it is easiest to see *lust* as an expression of distorted human sexuality, issues of power and control do not end there. In the context of human relationships, any situation where one person attempts to have power and control over another for their own personal gain is an example of the spiritual compulsion of *lust*. Mental, emotional, spiritual and physical abuse are all common examples. This kind of abuse is present in our workplace, within our families and in our intimate human relationships.

The temptation to indulge victimhood reveals the mirror image of compulsion and proves *lust* to be a two-way street. When we deny our own inner-knowing, our needs and desires, or our life's purpose in favor of another's demands, we have given our power away. In doing this, we have denied the very essence of our Self, and the oak tree that desires to be born within us has no choice but to die.

It is easiest to understand the spiritual compulsion of *lust* within the context of our interpersonal relationships, but how do we understand it in relation to our interior, personal journey to become the person God intended us to be? *Lust* from this perspective is related to our own compulsion to control the circumstances and outcome of our lives. It is this compulsion that Moses' mother finally had to face so that her son could reach the fullness of his human potential:

> *Pharaoh then commanded all his subjects, "Throw into the river every boy that is born to the Hebrews, but you may let all the girls live."*
>
> *Now a certain man of the house of Levi married a Levite woman, who conceived and bore a son. Seeing that he was a goodly child, she hid him for three months. When she could hide him no longer, she took a papyrus basket, daubed it with bitumen and pitch, and putting the child in it, placed it among the reeds on the river bank. His sister stationed herself at a distance to find out what would happen to him.*
>
> Exodus 1:22; 2:1-3

Integration

You are invited to enter into an experience of Imagination/Contemplation. (Imagination/Contemplation is a formal spiritual practice popularized by St. Ignatius of Loyola. Through this practice, we are invited to be open to the communication of Divine truth through our imagination and daydreaming.) Read through the above scripture passage slowly and prayerfully. You are now invited to imagine that you are Moses' mother. Imagine in detail the events unfolding from her perspective. Imagine every detail, allowing the scene and the events to unfold naturally. Be present to whatever is revealed, without being tempted to censor or critique. Pay special attention to the emotions you may be experiencing as the events unfold. Record your thoughts and reflections in your journal.

Reflect more deeply on how what came through in your imagining may be related to events in your own journey.

The story of Moses' birth perfectly illustrates the compulsion of *lust* and how we experience it in our personal journeys. In this case, it is Moses' mother who was tempted by, and eventually had to let go of, the compulsion to control the circumstances and outcome of a desperate situation so that the possibility might emerge for her son to reach his full potential.

Moses was born to a Hebrew family during a time of great political vulnerability. The new Pharaoh, unlike his compassionate predecessors, began to perceive the Hebrew presence as a threat to his power and control. He turned this fear against the Hebrews and began to enact laws that placed the Hebrews at his mercy. The Hebrews, who had previously enjoyed some sense of autonomy, had now become the slaves of the Egyptians. Persecution and slavery were not enough however, as the Pharaoh sought to further undermine the power and sheer numbers of the Hebrew people by issuing a decree that every male child should be executed.

Moses' mother, acting out of her own natural instinct, sought to protect her child from imminent death and did all she could to hide her son from the watchful eyes of the Egyptians, until his advancing age made this an impossible task. Moses' mother was now faced with a heart-rending decision: give her son up to the Egyptian soldiers, thus ensuring his death, or find some way to create another possibility. Her dilemma truly illustrates the *core fear* at work in this story, *the inability to bring forth life that persists* (Does she have the guts to risk his life to save him?) and its related compulsion, *lust* (Is she going to be give up control and let go of the outcome?). As every mother knows, the first choice would be almost unthinkable. Moses' mother sought another option. Letting go of her need to control the outcome, she placed her son in a basket, set him among the reeds and walked away. There was great risk in the outcome of this act: he could remain there at the riverbank and eventually succumb to starvation; the waters could sweep him away to an imminent, watery death; wild animals could find in him a delicious meal, *or* of least likelihood, some kind soul could discover the abandoned child and take pity on him. It was perhaps the final, least likely option that Moses' mother hoped for, but there was no way of guaranteeing that this would be the result. Taking a great leap of faith, Moses' mother placed the fate of her son in the hands of her God and placed him along the river bank, expecting never to see him again.

In this courageous act of selfless surrender, Moses' mother ensured that Moses would have the opportunity to reach the fullness of his human potential. As the story continues, Pharaoh's daughter discovered the boy and took pity on him. Moses' sister, Miriam, whose ingenuity led her to witness to the fate of her baby brother, intervened and facilitated the greatest blessing that her mother could have imagined. Moses' own mother was allowed to continue to nurture and care for her son until he was of an age (perhaps as old as five or seven) that he could return to his adoptive mother, in the palace of the Pharaoh. The unfolding of these events became the foundation upon which Moses' most authentic self could be allowed to emerge as the eventual liberator and lawgiver of the Hebrew people. If Moses' mother had continued to cling to her desire for control over the fate of her young child, perhaps none of these dreams would have been realized. It was only in surrendering to the providence of her Divine Source that Moses' fate was sealed.

What was true for Moses' mother is equally true for us. How often do we cling to what we know, to what is familiar, to the safety of our own ideas and visions for our life, instead of surrendering to the possibility of something new, unwilling to go out on a limb and trust that our Divine Source might have a better plan? The truth is that there is a Divine Source that knows what is in our highest good and sees within us our potential greatness. The God of our understanding seeks to be expressed in and through us and in that expression, desires for us to know the peace and love that is our highest nature—our Oneness with God. It is our ego, our fears, our attachments and our need to control that stand in the way of our ability to allow God to freely live and find its expression through us. As such, our highest potential is rarely, if ever, realized. It is in surrendering our need to control and letting go of what we know, that God is able to freely move in and through us, carrying us to the place of our greatest potential. It is here that we know peace, love, and freedom, realizing the blessings of our God that are far beyond what we could possibly have created for ourselves.

EASTERN MEDICINE AS A TOOL FOR HEALING— THE SACRAL CHAKRA

The *sacral chakra*, located in the center of our belly, just below the navel, is the energy center that governs and reflects the interior procreative drive. The drive to continue the species, as well as the drive to be an open vessel through which God can be revealed through our own unique gifts, are related to the *sacral chakra*.

Physically, the *sacral chakra* is directly related to the state of health of all organs of procreation. The sexual organs of both men and women are directly responsible for the action of continuing the species. Any dysfunction related to our sexual organs may be reflective of an unhealthy relationship with the procreative and creative drive. If we are indulging the compulsion of *lust* out of the spiritual fear that *we will not be able to bring forth life that will persist*, we will sometimes experience the physical results of this through erectile dysfunction, frigidity, infertility, premature ejaculation, etc. If we are suffering from any of the physical, sexual dysfunctions, it may be helpful to look at our creative needs—are they being met?

Are we seeking to name and claim our gifts and our own personal needs? Are we in touch with the fullness of our human potential and are we working toward allowing that to be made manifest?

It is not a coincidence that men and women who have been survivors of sexual abuse often experience diseases of the reproductive organs: testicular, prostate, uterine and ovarian cancers are just a few examples. Issues of sexual dysfunction are also common among survivors of sexual abuse. States of disease in these areas are even more common among those who have not sought healing for the abuse that they have suffered. When someone infringes on another's freedom and boundaries in such a violent manner, it has dramatic and sometimes irreversible effects. Healing of this type of abuse requires support in many different areas and can take years, even a lifetime to complete.

On an emotional level, when we deny the drive within us to bring forth life (physically and metaphorically), we experience a kind of emotional death. When we give up our own needs and desires for others, the part of us that seeks to find its expression eventually gives up, the effect of which is the sensation that our spirit has shriveled up and died. We become despondent, depressed and listless. Emotional depression (in contrast to clinical depression which is a brain chemical imbalance) is frequently related to our inability to name and claim our unique giftedness. When we deny the physical or creative life that seeks to be born from within us, a part of us feels as if it has died. This kind of emotional depression also emerges when we find ourselves engaged in relationships that are centered in power and control. When the other party seeks to maintain power and control over us and we are without the inner strength to resist their efforts, we will often sink into a state of emotional depression, surrendering to the power that we perceive to be greater than our own.

When we resist the movement of the Divine within us, seeking to control our own destinies or the destinies of others, the *sacral chakra* will reflect a state of disharmony and disease. When we deny our needs as well as our gifts, we will find that we suffer. It is this state of control and denial that is most commonly reflected in the negative emotional, mental and physical states associated with the *sacral chakra*.

When we are allowing ourselves to be open to the flow of the Divine within us, allowing this Divine energy to move us toward the fulfillment of our most authentic selves, the *sacral chakra* will be in a state of balance and openness. When we allow this energy to reveal our inner gifts and work toward allowing these gifts to be cultivated and shared, the *sacral chakra* will remain healthy. When we allow this Divine energy to help us name and claim our needs, ensuring that our personal needs are being met, we remain in harmony with this chakra and move effortlessly toward the fulfillment of our soul's purpose, enjoying the peace and joy of living in that state of fulfillment.

When the creative energy within us seeks to be expressed, we often have no choice but to respond to its promptings. Unfortunately, we frequently falsely perceive that we do not have the gifts to allow that life to find its expression. Additionally, bringing forth this new life often means that something else must die, or be set aside. As such, we find ourselves resisting the movement of that new life within us. Fortunately, we cannot deny this creative call for long without experiencing the pain of repression. To put it in theistic terms, God is seeking to be expressed in and through us, through the discovery, cultivation and sharing of our own unique giftedness. Like the acorn that has no choice but to become the oak, we too have no choice but to become what God intended. This energy of God's desire is persistent and consistent and will badger us until we surrender to God's providence. Denial of this inner call results in physical, emotional and mental distress—not as a form of punishment—but as a natural result of denying our true nature. Working toward fulfillment of revelation, God is a nag. When we deny this creative energy, we feel a sensation of impatient desperation. It is only in giving honor to and freeing that creative energy within us that we can find the peaceful fulfillment that God intended.

Integration

In Eastern medicine, the creative energy within us that seeks to find its expression through us is envisioned as a snake. This snake lies coiled within us near the base of the spine and as we work toward becoming the fulfillment of our most authentic selves, this snake uncoils, moving up through our being until it reaches the heavens through the crown of our head. As a meditation, take 20–30 minutes in silence envisioning this snake coiled within you, resting in the center of your belly. Allow yourself to be open to the presence of this creative energy and allow yourself to listen to how it may be speaking to you. Assure the snake protection and safety and invite it to begin to unfurl within you. Be mindful of how comfortable you are with allowing the snake to uncoil within you. Pay attention to any thoughts and emotions that may surface during this visualization.

So far, our journey to Authentic Freedom has introduced us to the *core wound*—the false sense of separation from God, and that led us to discover the second manifestation of this wound in the fear that *we are unable to bring for life that persists*. This fear is then demonstrated through a set of compulsions and behaviors (such as an overly strong attachment to dominate other people or situations, or control outcomes, or an inability to risk moving forward) experienced as *lust*, which then perpetuates an imbalance in the *sacral chakra* and all the organs to which its energy flows. We are now ready for the next step in the Authentic Freedom process: we move toward exploring the healing truth that gives release to the fear of not being able to bring forth life that persists and helps us move toward fully embracing our magnificence. This healing vehicle is the sacred truth *that you are uniquely gifted to reveal God in the world.*

SACRED TRUTH—YOU ARE CO-CREATOR WITH GOD AND WHEN YOU SURRENDER TO THIS PROCESS, TOGETHER YOU BRING FORTH LIFE THAT PERSISTS

It is in embracing the second sacred truth that we are freed of the fear *we are unable to bring forth life that will persist* and its resulting compulsion of *lust.* It is the truth that *we are co-creators with God and when we surrender to this process, together we bring forth life that persists* that Paul reveals in his first letter to the Corinthians.

> *There are different kinds of gifts, but the same Spirit. There are different kinds of service, but the same Lord. There are different kinds of working, but the same God works all of them in all people.*
>
> *Now to each one the manifestation of the Spirit is given for the common good. To one there is given through the Spirit the message of wisdom, to another the message of knowledge by means of the same Spirit, to another faith by the same Spirit, to another gifts of healing by that one Spirit, to another miraculous powers, to another prophecy, to another distinguishing between spirits, to another speaking in different kinds of tongues, and to still another the interpretation of tongues. All these are the work of one and the same Spirit, and the Spirit gives them to each one just as the Spirit determines.*
>
> *The body is a unit, though it is made up of many parts; and though all its parts are many, they form one body. So it is*

with Christ. For we were all baptized by one Spirit into one body—whether Jews or Greeks, slave or free—and we were all given the one Spirit to drink.

Now you are the body of Christ, and each one of you is a part of it!

1 Corinthians 12:1-13, 27

Each and every one of us is uniquely gifted to be a vessel through which God is revealed in the world. It is this truth that we are invited to explore, discern, embrace, cultivate, nurture and share openly. We are gifted to reveal God through our gifts as teacher, healer, nurturer, lover, helper, guide, muse, friend, beauty bringer, peace giver, justice keeper, social activist, counselor, etc. etc. etc. The ways in which we are gifted to reveal God are limitless. In this reading from Paul's letter to the Corinthians, we are reminded of the depth of this truth. In the eyes of God, there is no gift that goes unnoticed. While it is easier to accept that God is revealed through us in the things we are proud of, it is far more difficult to accept that God is also revealed through what we perceive to be our greatest weaknesses—or through those in our society whom we perceive of lesser value. In fact, it is often through our perceived weaknesses that God is most profoundly revealed.

On the contrary, those parts of the body that seem to be weaker are indispensable, and the parts that we think are less honorable we treat with special honor. And the parts that are unpresentable are treated with special modesty, while our presentable parts need no special treatment. But God has combined the members of the body and has given greater honor to the parts that lacked it, so that there should be no division in the body, but that its parts should have equal concern for each other.

1 Corinthians 12:22-25

When we participate in the movement of the Holy Spirit in helping to bring about the fullness of the kingdom of God by openly sharing our gifts, we are *Being the Body of Christ*. It is only through our full participation in this call that the work Jesus began 2000 years ago can be made complete. Embracing the truth of our unique giftedness moves us individually and collectively toward knowing the fullness of God's peace, love and joy, right here, right now. It is for this purpose that God gave us life and it is to this end that we are compelled to act. Like the acorn that has no choice but to become an oak, we have no choice but to become the person we were intended to become. The good news is that like the acorn, becoming the person we were intended to be requires no direct effort on our part—we need simply surrender to the process that God will unfold in us. It is this truth that Jesus speaks of in the following passage from Mark's gospel:

> *Jesus said, "This is how it is with the Kingdom of God; it is as if a man were to scatter seed on the land and would sleep and rise night and day and the seed would sprout and grown, he knows not how. Of its own accord the land yields fruit, first the blade, then the ear, then the full grain in the ear. And when the grain is ripe, he wields the sickle at once, for the harvest has come."*
>
> Mark 4:26-27

It is in surrendering to this process that we can truly bring forth life that will persist. It is in being open to allowing God to reveal God's self through our gifts as well as our perceived weaknesses that the fullness of God's dream can be made complete. In this way, the life that we are called to bring forth will persist.

HOLY VIRTUE—FORTITUDE

Allowing ourselves to hear, accept and nurture this creative voice requires great courage. To be fully present to this voice, we have to be willing to let go of what we currently know to embrace a life as yet revealed. Accomplishing this task provides for us an opportunity to experience the virtue of *fortitude.*

Fortitude is the virtue that allows us to accept the grief of losing the life we have come to know so that we can move through the process of transformation and experience the promise of new life. It is this experience of new life that inspires us, strengthens us, emboldens us and keeps us going. Only in surrendering to God and allowing God to be fully revealed through us can *fortitude* be made known. It is here, in this process of embracing the promise of authentic freedom that new life is revealed to us, each and every day.

CHAPTER FIVE

You Can Do It!

Behold, you will conceive in your womb, and bear a son, and you shall name him Jesus. But Mary said to the angel, "How can this be, since I have no relations with a man?" And the angel said to her in reply, "The Holy Spirit will come upon you, and the power of the Most High will overshadow you . . . for nothing will be impossible for God."

Luke 1:31, 34–35a, 37

God calls each and every one of us into a life of peace, love and joy where we are content in knowing that God alone is the source of our desires and the agent of our transformation. Embracing the life of authentic freedom means that we know God, we know ourselves and we are aware of the gifts God has given us and how we are called to share those gifts in the world. Moreover, we know that we are free to share these gifts in the world and we do so generously. In this act of naming, cultivating and sharing our gifts, we become co-creators with God, helping to bring forth the fullness of the kingdom. Unfortunately, for most of us, when we begin to hear this voice, and through the process of attempting to fully embrace and live as our most authentic self, our unanimous response is, "I can't". "I can't be and live as the person God created me to be because . . . (add your list of excuses . . .)"

THE FEAR—I CAN'T

The good news is that we are not alone in this fear. Scripture is filled with the stories of prophets and holy people who, when faced with the call to share their gifts in the world, responded with a resounding "I can't." Noah tells God he can't build the ark because people will think him crazy. Sarah can't because she is too old. In the book of Exodus, we see Moses bargaining with God over all the reasons he can't lead the Israelites out of Egypt. The people say David can't be king because he is the youngest son and a mere shepherd. Jeremiah can't because he is too young. Isaiah can't because he is a sinful man. Joseph can't take Mary into his house because she has sinned against him. Peter can't because he is scared. Over and over, when faced with the invitation to become a vessel through which God's peace, love and joy are revealed in the world, human beings run the other way, thinking themselves unable to complete the tasks God has offered them. Falsely believing that our perceived inadequacies or our external circumstances could hinder the work of God, we respond, "I can't."

As much as we would like to embrace and live as the person God has created us to be, a distortion inside tells us something else. This voice of discord, also known as the false self, reminds us of all the ways we cannot be our most authentic self. This voice of discord is the loud and obtrusive voice of temptation. It is the "great obstacle" doing all it can to keep us from remembering the truth of Oneness, so that we can forever wallow in the pits of separation, never attaining the fullness of our potential as vessels of God's love, peace and joy in the world.

Temptation is a stage in the spiritual process that we all must face. It is the obstacle within that causes us to say, "I can't." Each and every one of us has faced this obstacle, as have all the holy men and women who have gone before us. Most notably, is Jesus' own temptation in the desert.

> *It happened in those days that Jesus came from Nazareth of Galilee and was baptized in the Jordan by John. On coming up out of the water he saw the heavens being torn open and the Spirit, like a dove, descending upon him. And a voice came from the heavens, "You are my beloved Son; with you I am well pleased."*
>
> *At once the Spirit drove him out into the desert, and he remained in the desert for forty days, tempted by Satan. He was among wild beasts, and the angels ministered to him.*
>
> Mark 1:9–13

Integration

Take a few minutes to prayerfully reflect on the scripture passage above. Reflect especially on the moment that Jesus hears the voice from heaven proclaiming, "You are my beloved Son; with you I am well pleased." Put yourself in Jesus' shoes. In your journal, write about what it would feel like to hear those words being spoken directly to you by God:

- You are God's son/daughter! What does that mean?
- What are the implications of this awareness?
- What are all the things you could now do as the Son/Daughter of God?
- What are the good things you could do with this awareness?
- How might you be tempted to abuse this power?

The baptism by John in the Jordan River represents an important transition in the spiritual journey of Jesus. Presumably, having spent the preceding 20 years working as a carpenter with Joseph, Jesus hears a voice from the heavens proclaiming him to be the Son of God. This is life-altering information! What does it mean to be the Son of God and what will this mean in his life? Jesus could not simply return to Nazareth to build furniture. He had to spend time figuring out what it means to be the Son of God. Mark's gospel portrays the profound urgency of Jesus' foray into the desert: *"At once (or immediately) the Spirit drove him out into the desert . . ."* (Some translations even say that "he fled into the desert."). This time of retreat could not wait. The revelation of being the Son of God was too great to ignore! Leaving everything behind, Jesus went into the desert to connect with the fullness of this truth. The journey into the desert became Jesus' opportunity to discern the meaning of this revelation and its implications in his life.

Ultimately, Jesus' baptism and 40-day desert retreat served as the final preparation for Jesus' entry into public ministry. Discovering his true nature, Jesus now had to face the fears that would prevent him from living this truth. The gospel of Matthew elaborates on the nature of these fears:

Then Jesus was led by the Spirit into the desert to be tempted by the devil. He fasted for forty days and forty nights, and afterwards he was hungry. The tempter approached and said to him, "If you are the Son of God, command that these stones become loaves of bread." He said in reply, "It is written: 'One does not live by bread alone but by every word that comes forth from the mouth of God.'

Then the devil took him to the holy city, and made him stand on the parapet of the temple, and said to him, "If you are the Son of God, throw yourself down. For it is written: 'He will command his angels concerning you' and 'with their hands

they will support you, lest you dash your foot against a stone.'"
Jesus answered him, "Again it is written, 'You shall not put the
Lord your God to the test.'

Then the devil took him up to a very high mountain, and
showed him all the kingdoms of the world in their magnificence,
and he said to him, "All these I shall give to you, if you will
prostrate yourself and worship me." At this, Jesus said to him,
"Get away, Satan! It is written: 'The Lord, your God, shall
you worship and him alone shall you serve.' Then the devil left
him and, behold, angels came and ministered to him.

Matthew 4:1-11

Integration

Take a few minutes and prayerfully read through the scripture passage
above. In your journal, write about the temptations Jesus faced. In
particular, reflect on how you have experienced these temptations
in your own life:

- Where have you experienced the desire for material
  wealth, power and control?
- How have these desires become an obstacle to experiencing
  peace, joy and love in your life?
- What other obstacles have you experienced to authentic
  freedom?

Jesus discovered through careful discernment and prayer that
accepting his true nature meant he had to let go of all of the fears
and ego attachments that might impede his ability to live the
freedom that God now offered to him as the Son of God. He even
had to let go of the fear of death. He had to release his attachment

to control and he had to set free any temptation to use his power for his own benefit or to place himself in a position of dominance over others. Through the temptation in the desert, Jesus was able to release every notion within him that prevented him from freely and openly living the life God had intended. This experience also served as a model for future temptations that Jesus might face in his own journey toward authentic freedom. In successfully thwarting temptation, Jesus provides a model that we too can follow when faced with the inner obstacle that seeks to prevent us from being the person God intended us to be.

SATAN AND THE ROLE OF TEMPTATION

In Jesus' temptation in the desert, the obstacle that he faced is given the name "Satan," a Hebrew word that means *adversary* or *obstacle*. From this perspective, Satan is that which prevents us from remembering the love that is God and from remembering this love as the truth of who we are. Satan is the fear within us that prevents us from living and being the truth that God intended us to be. Satan imprisons us in the false perception of separation from God and one another. Satan in this respect is another word for fear, false-self or ego. Residing within our minds, in the fears that come out of the *core spiritual wound*, Satan is no more the "man with pitchfork in hand" than God is the "old man in the sky."

When we allow ourselves to be paralyzed by the fear of temptation and evil, we are prevented from embracing the authentic freedom that is God's intention for our lives. We are unable to discover, embrace and enjoy the peace, the love and the joy that God has promised we would have. When we recognize evil and temptation for what they are—obstacles to a life of authentic freedom—we empower ourselves to approach these demons as opportunities to embrace the peace and love of God, rather than falling back into the morass of *I can't*. With God's help, we are able to face our fears, and work toward transforming and giving them release so that we can embrace and live as our most authentic selves.

It is God's desire that we allow ourselves to be vessels through which God's creative vision can be made manifest and that in doing so, we become co-creators with God. This desire is a vibrant energy that lives within us and compels us to seek out a deeper understanding of God and ourselves. Growth in this knowledge provides the revelation of our own unique gifts and how we are being called to use them to reveal God's love in the world. When this Divine creative spark rises up within us, it blazes into a force that is to be reckoned with, for it is an energy that is dynamic and purposeful; unable to be thwarted. This creative energy will have its way, regardless of what we decide to do with it. Amy Grant calls this energy "The Power:"

> *The Power touches me*
> *The Power helps me see*
> *The Power holds my hand*
> *The Power drives me crazy*
> (*The Power* by Amy Grant from the album, **House of Love**)

This Power has no patience for *I can't*. When challenged with our fears, it does not walk away in defeat. Rather, it hounds us internally, until we find a way to give this Power its voice. When we ignore or repress this Power as it seeks to be known through us, we are tempted to give into the compulsion of *wrath*, otherwise known as anger.

DEADLY COMPULSION—WRATH

Wrath, the resulting compulsion of the fear *I can't*, has many faces: the self-motivating anger that compels us to get off our butts and respond to the call of empowerment; the bitter anger that surfaces due to a loss; the rage that boils inside when we feel we have no control; the deadly anger that destroys everyone in its path; the anger of vengeance, retaliation, spite, resentment and malice. One of the most pervasive and unrecognized faces of anger is as an expression of grief.

ANGER AND GRIEF

Grief is a gift given to us by our Divine Creator that serves to help us heal from the many losses and deaths we experience in our lives. We experience grief in the face of the loss of a loved one or someone important to us. We experience grief when we receive bad news about our own health such as in a terminal diagnosis. More subtly, we experience grief at any moment of loss or change in our lives—when we lose a job or our business fails, when our children grow up and go off to college, when we change jobs or residences, when we celebrate our birthdays, when we notice our bodies don't work the same way as they once did. In any of these moments of loss—and millions of others like them—grief surfaces as a tool for healing so that we may prepare ourselves for the new life that is waiting to come into our experience.

Unfortunately, we live in a culture that does not honor grief in this way, and so we lack the understanding that would help us accept grief as a natural and healthy process. It often feels as if grief is not allowed. When we experience a loss or death, we are told, "Get over it! Get on with your life. Move on!" While validation of our grieving process is often not forthcoming, the anger that accompanies grief is flat-out ignored. To make matters worse, our culture does not provide effective tools for moving through the anger so that the grieving process may unfold. As a result, we feel as if we have to ignore the faces of grief—anger, depression, denial and bargaining. Repression of grief only serves to lengthen the process, delaying healing and an openness to the new life that will be found on the other side of the loss. As Elizabeth Kubler-Ross revealed in her studies of grieving, all of these faces of grief are natural and provide effective tools through which healing can begin.

Another common face of *wrath* is the anger we experience when we perceive the creative energy ("the Power") within us as being hindered. When we perceive that there is force outside of us—an individual, our life circumstance, our status, position, power, lack of time, money, energy, resources or support—that could interfere with our ability to be the person God has called us to be, we feel rage.

And yet another aspect of *wrath* would be that which we experience in the face of injustice. Scripture gives us an illustration of this kind of anger:

> *Then Jesus entered the temple area and proceeded to drive out those who were selling things, saying to them, "It is written, 'My house shall be a house of prayer, but you have made it a den of thieves.'"*
>
> Luke 19:45-46

Jesus acted in anger out of a sense of injustice. The temple, a place he considered sacred, had become desecrated by the money changers and the marketers who were selling objects for sacrifice. Jesus recognized that these businesses were taking advantage of the people and were profiting from what was required of the people by religious law. Jesus become indignant at this injustice and launched his own nonviolent demonstration.

In our own journeys, it is not uncommon—in fact, it is correct—to experience anger in the face of injustices such as poverty, war, segregation, discrimination, political violence, and the inequitable distribution of resources, medical care and education. There is no reason, at our current level of intellectual and spiritual evolution, for injustice to remain in our world. Unfortunately, most of us are still operating out of the *core spiritual wound*, and until this wound is healed within ourselves and within our world, injustices will remain. Anger is a natural emotion in the face of injustice, especially when it feels we are powerless to help. It is what we do with this anger that determines if it is the healthy, or the unhealthy manifestation of *wrath*.

When, in the face of injustice, we choose a nonviolent response to our anger, it can become a powerful tool for empowerment and change. The civil rights movement led by Dr. Martin Luther King Jr., is one such example, as is the suffragette movement of the early 20th century that eventually gave women the right to vote. In this way, anger becomes a great source of motivation, compelling us to move out of our complacency into a state of empowered activism. Sometimes is takes a good dose of blatant anger to get us off our butts and working toward positive change.

However, when, in the face of injustice, we choose a violent response to anger, it becomes unhealthy. Anger becomes a powerful weapon of destruction when it is projected outward and acted out through violence, or when it is turned inward where it is fostered as resentment, hatred and disgust. Healthy, loving relationships have been destroyed when one or both parties have chosen to blame the other person for their perceived limitations. Failing to recognize our own responsibility in working toward the fulfillment of our authentic selves, we often lash out at those closest to us, thinking they are to blame for our anger and fear. When we do this on a global level, our *wrath* leads to the most vividly unhealthy expressions of retaliation, revenge, terrorism and war. The invitation in the face of injustice is to embrace our anger and look for healthy ways in which we can work toward a positive change, without doing violence to ourselves or others.

Studying the subtle nuances of *wrath* (anger) helps differentiate its potential as a tool of empowerment from its potential as a weapon of mass destruction. It is important to understand this distinction if we ever hope to more fully live as the person God intended us to be.

Integration

Take some time to reflect on your own experience with *wrath*. Give special attention to the reflection questions below:

- What is your personal relationship with anger?
- Is anger an acceptable emotion and how do you respond to it?
- How do you express your anger?
- When have you experienced a death or significant loss in your life?
- Where have you experienced anger in the face of this loss?
- How did you respond to that anger?
- Where have you felt anger in the face of perceived blocks to your freedom to be and live as your most authentic self?
- What did you do with that anger?
- Did you suppress it, harbor it, turn it inward, project it on to another, turn it into resentment?
- How do you respond to injustice?
- What are some positive things you could do to stand up against injustice without resorting to violence?
- What are your thoughts about revenge, retaliation, retribution?
- How might you respond in a way that would support non-violence?

EASTERN MEDICINE AS A TOOL FOR HEALING— THE SOLAR PLEXUS

It is not always easy to recognize the fear *I can't* and its resulting compulsion, *wrath*, as active in our lives. Turning to knowledge of the chakras and their corresponding functions gives us additional tools for recognizing physical, emotional and mental symptoms of this fear manifesting within us. *I can't be and live as my most authentic self* can be recognized through greater awareness of the energy center (chakra) known as the *solar plexus.*

The *solar plexus*, located in the soft spot, just below where our ribs separate, is the center responsible for assimilation and trans-formation. Assimilation is the process through which our spiritual, emotional, mental and physical bodies absorb (take in) what is life-giving. On a physical level, this is specifically related to digestion and the absorption of nutrients. Transformation is the process through which we are able to change the composition of, and give release to, that with is no longer life-giving. On a physical level, this is the process through which that which is not assimilated is transformed into liquid and solid waste. To understand how this process works, we need only look to the element of fire that is related to this en-ergy center.

Fire is the most crucial element necessary for our physical sur-vival as human beings. Without fire in the form of the sun, we would not have life. Fire provides light, warmth, protection and safety. Fire provided primitive man the opportunity to purify and transform food that would not otherwise be safe to eat. As much as it is nec-essary for survival, fire is also potentially dangerous. While fire has the power to give life, it also has the power to destroy. Volcanoes, lightning strikes and forest fires are all examples of the potentially destructive action of fire. What we sometimes neglect to observe, however, is that even in its most destructive form, fire yields the promise of new life. This is its transformational power. As fire de-stroys that which is dead or no longer supportive of new growth, it clears the way for new life to take root and transforms that which is being destroyed into the fertile ground in which new life can be supported in its growth. This process of assimilation, destruction and new life is the lesson of the *solar plexus*.

On a physical level, the *solar plexus* governs our digestion. The stomach, pancreas, spleen, liver, gallbladder and small intestine are the organs necessary for this process. Through the taking in of food and the digestive process, we are able to absorb the nutrients that give us life, and give release to that which does not. It is the fire in our digestive system that allows this process to unfold. Putting this process in the context of authentic freedom, we can look to ailments in the digestive system as possible manifestations of the fear *I can't* and its resulting compulsion of *wrath*. When we are deeply rooted in this fear and it is not healed on the spiritual, emotional or mental level, it will eventually manifest in the physical. Ulcers, reflux disease, nausea, hepatitis, cirrhosis, gall stones, mononucleosis and immune system disorders may be the physical manifestation of this fear left unhealed.

The primary mental manifestation of the fear *I can't* is worry. Worry is the constant examination of and attention to fear, frequently experienced as obsessive thoughts. It is in this way that the *solar plexus* is said to be connected with the mind.

Emotionally, the unhealed fear, *I can't*, is related to all issues of anger and resentment. In Chinese medicine, the liver, gallbladder and spleen are said to be the organs in which our anger resides. We have all heard the sayings: "That really galled me," or "I needed to vent my spleen." These are prime examples of our intuitive awareness of the intimate connection between these organs and their emotional components. Anger and its cousins, impatience and irritability, are oftentimes related to our fear that *we cannot be and live as our most authentic selves*. Resentment, revenge and wrath are the destructive ways that we project this anger either upon ourselves or another.

Integration

When dealing with the fear *I can't*, guided meditation becomes a powerful tool for healing. Using the scripture passage below, imagine that you are Isaiah. Invite God to reveal to you the things within yourself that are no longer life-giving and that are standing in the way of your ability to be and live as your most authentic self. Imagine the seraphim removing an ember from the fire and bringing it to those areas in need of healing and release. Allow the burning ember to transform and release those things within you that are coming out of the fear "I can't."

> *In the year king Uzziah died, I saw the Lord seated on a high and lofty throne, with the train of his garment filling the temple. Then I said, "Woe is me, I am doomed! For I am a man of unclean lips, living among a people of unclean lips; yet my eyes have seen the King, the Lord of hosts!" Then one of the seraphim flew to me, holding an ember which he had taken with tongs from the altar. He touched my mouth with it. "See," he said, "now that this has touched your lips, your wickedness is removed, your sin purged." Then I heard the voice of the Lord saying, "Whom shall I send? Who will go for us?" "Here I am;" I said, "send me!" And he replied, "Go . . ."*
>
> Isaiah 6:1, 5-9

The fear *I can't*, is the third expression of the unhealed *core wound*—the false perception of separation from God. This fear and its resulting compulsion, *wrath*, manifest themselves in the *solar plexus* and all of the organs through which its energy flows. Our awareness (recognition/acknowledgement) of this fear, its compulsion and its related physical, emotional and mental manifestations, prepares us to open our hearts and minds to the promise of God's healing through the *third sacred truth*, which can serve as an antidote to the anger, resentment and anxiety that occur when we forget that there is no power greater than that which creates and sustains each of us on our quest to live as unique expressions of God.

SACRED TRUTH—THERE IS NOTHING OUTSIDE OF YOU THAT CAN KEEP YOU FROM LIVING FREELY AS YOUR MOST AUTHENTIC SELF—THE PERSON GOD MADE YOU TO BE

For most of our human journey, we look outside of ourselves for fulfillment. We expect people and objects outside of us to be the source of our happiness. When we find ourselves unfulfilled, unsatisfied, stifled and burdened, we suspect that someone or something outside of us is the source of our discontent. We are forever projecting credit for happiness and blame for unhappiness outside of ourselves, rarely accepting responsibility for our own fulfillment. The hard truth is that the only source of fulfillment is within us in our sacred connection with God. As it is said, "God alone is the source of our desire and the agent of our transformation." Lasting fulfillment will not be found elsewhere.

This is especially true in our journey toward becoming our most authentic self, the person God created us to be. One of our most difficult tasks is accepting the gift that is calling to be brought forth into the world through each of us, and providing the resources this gift needs in order to be revealed. We come up with all kinds of excuses, most of which we want to believe are someone else's fault, for why we cannot be or live as the person God created us to be. The truth that we struggle to believe is that *there is nothing outside of us that can prevent us from being the person God created us to be*. The only thing that can prevent us from being our most authentic self is us. What we most frequently forget is that with God all things are possible. Mary, the mother of Jesus, was reminded of this truth in her encounter with the angel Gabriel:

In the sixth month, the angel Gabriel was sent from God to a town of Galilee called Nazareth, to a virgin betrothed to a man named Joseph of the house of David, and the virgin's name was Mary. And coming to her, he said, "Hail favored one! The Lord is with you." But she was greatly troubled at what was said and pondered what sort of greeting this might be. Then the angel said to her, "Do not be afraid, Mary, for you have found favor with God. Behold, you will conceive in your womb and bear a son, and you shall name him Jesus." But Mary said to the angel, "How can this be, since I have no relations with a man?" And the angel said to her in reply, "The Holy Spirit will come upon you, and the power of the Most High will overshadow you. Therefore the child to be born will be called holy, the Son of God. And behold, Elizabeth, your relative, has also conceived a son in her old age, and this is the sixth month for her who was called barren; for nothing will be impossible for God." Mary said, "Behold, I am the handmaid of the Lord. May it be done to me according to your word."

Luke 1:26–31, 34–38a

Integration

You are invited to enter into an experience of Imagination/ Contemplation. Imagine yourself to be the child, Mary. She is 13 years old and has this encounter with a spiritual messenger. Place yourself in her shoes as you allow the scene to unfold. Record your thoughts and reflections, being mindful especially of the fears and doubts that may surface.

Through the gift of modern-day scripture scholarship, we have some additional information about the cultural practices in the time that Mary lived to add details to this story. In most likelihood, Mary was a girl between the ages of twelve and fourteen. Mary was legally contracted to marry Joseph, but had not yet shared the marriage bed. To have been found pregnant out of wedlock by a person other than her betrothed would have brought shame upon Mary and her parent's household. Joseph, as her betrothed had the legal right to have her stoned and killed for being found pregnant by someone other than him. Mary was at great risk in saying yes to the angel's invitation. She risked being ostracized by her family and killed by her husband. And yet, Mary believed in the angel's words that *with God all things would be possible.* In accepting this call, Mary became the vessel through which one of humanities greatest teachers would be born. Mary allowed God to reveal God's self through her in the most amazing way, and in doing so, lived freely as her most authentic self. This is the invitation we are all called to embrace. How are we being called to birth God's love in the world and how can we trust that there is nothing outside of us that can stand in the way of our ability to do so? How can we remember the truth that *with God, all things are possible*?

The prophet Jeremiah had an opportunity to explore the answer to these questions in his own life.

Call of Jeremiah:
The word of the Lord came to me thus:
Before I formed you in the womb I knew you,
Before you were born I dedicated you,
A prophet to the nations I anointed you.
"Ah, Lord God!" I said, "I know not how to speak; I am too young."
But the Lord answered me,
Say not, "I am too young."
To whomever I send you, you shall go;
Whatever I command you, you shall speak.

Have no fear before them, because I am with you to deliver you,
  said the Lord.
Then the Lord extended his hand and touched my mouth,
  saying,
See, I place my words in your mouth!"

Jeremiah 1:4-9

Jeremiah learned the truth that the source of spiritual liberation and empowerment is God. In spite of Jeremiah's perceived limitations, God was able to work in and through him to reveal God's message of liberation to the Hebrew people. When we adhere to this truth, we find that through prayer and careful discernment that we are led to spiritual liberation. No longer imprisoned by the fears and false perceptions that lead us into falsely believing that anything can stand in the way of God's truth, we discover that through God's healing, we are able to truly live as our most authentic selves, embracing the unique giftedness given to us by God and sharing those gifts freely and generously in the world.

Integration

Take a few moments to record your thoughts and reactions to the truth that *with God all things are possible.* Record your own doubts, fears, etc., regarding this truth.

HOLY VIRTUE—MERCY

As we grow in our ability to face the inner voice that says *I can't* and move toward embracing the truth that *nothing exists outside of us that can prevent us from experiencing our Divine authenticity,* we are profoundly transformed, and we begin to understand the virtue of *mercy. Mercy* is the gift that we offer to ourselves and to others that allows for the vulnerability of our human nature. Recognizing that none of us are exempt from the voice of the ego that tries to tell us we are anything less than magnificent, we begin to understand that it is OK to be human and natural to struggle on our spiritual path. We are then invited to give ourselves and others the gift of patience. Through patience and acceptance, we find forgiveness for ourselves for falling short of our own expectations, and for our perception of others' expectations of us. At the same time, we find that we are able to let go of our expectations and judgment of others. When we allow *mercy* to expand our ability to accept and forgive, we progress along the initiatory path and recollection of our most authentic selves.

CHAPTER SIX

Love Is Who You Are

God is love, and whoever remains in love remains in God and God in him. In this is love brought to perfection among us, that we have confidence on the day of judgment because as he is, so are we in this world. There is no fear in love, but perfect love drives out fear because fear has to do with punishment, and so one who fears is not yet perfect in love. We love because God loved us first.

1 John 4:16b-19

THE FEAR—I AM NOT LOVED

Christine stepped into my office feeling devastated, shocked, depressed and desperately alone, three weeks after her husband of 40 years left her for another woman. She had grown up believing that she had to earn love by sacrificing her own needs for the benefit of others. As a homemaker who had wholeheartedly supported the dreams of her husband and children, she had never taken the time to cultivate her own gifts or interests. When her husband deserted her, she was left to wonder, "How could he do this to me after all I've done for him? Why could I not do enough to make him love me?" Through her husband's departure, she felt completely rejected and confused. Christine had forgotten the truth that love is the very nature of who she is and not something that can be denied, nor does it have to be earned.

Each and every one of us can relate to Christine in some way. Living out of the false perception of separation from God, we have embraced the fourth core fear that *I am not loved*—a fear that stems from the idea that love is a commodity to be bought, sold, earned or given with strings attached; that love can be denied us and that we have the power to deny others of the love that they are. Love has been reduced to a pawn in the game of life.

These and other false perceptions about love come out of our individual and collective unhealed *core wound*. Falsely believing ourselves to be separate from God, we feel deprived of the love that we are. We project this feeling of deprivation on to our human relationships, expecting them to provide the love we feel we are missing. We seek love through the approval of others, through friendships and through the never-ending quest for the perfect partner who will promise to make us whole. Because we continue to suffer the unhealed *core wound*—the false perception of separation from God, our human experience of love is conditional, jealous and fickle. Knowing nothing else, we then project our distorted sense of love onto God and experience God's love as conditional, jealous and fickle, as well.

For those raised in the Judeo–Christian tradition, Scripture illustrates this tendency to project our human experience of love onto God: God becomes a tyrant, who is to be feared, and whose love is conditional at best; God becomes the punisher, who condemns us with suffering when we disappoint "him." These distortions then demand that we "earn back" God's love and approval so that we can return to the paradise that was deprived of us as a result of the "disobedience" of our first human parents. If we do not appease this angry God in our earthly life, we are damned to spend an eternity in hell.

The story of The Fall of Man is a fantastic illustration of how we have lived out this projection.

> *Then the Lord God said: "See! The man has become like one of us, knowing what is good and what is bad! Therefore, he must not be allowed to put out his hand to take fruit from the tree of life also, and thus eat of it and live forever." The Lord God therefore banished him from the Garden of Eden, to till the ground from which he had been taken. When he expelled the man, he settled him east of the Garden of Eden; and he stationed the cherubim and the fiery sword, to guard the way to the tree of life.*
>
> Genesis 3:22-24

Religious doctrine, practices and structures have been created to reinforce these images of a judgmental, punitive God. In the Catholic Christian experience, the doctrine of original sin was inspired by a literal interpretation of this story, and continues to be used as a way to manipulate the fearful believers who struggle to earn the approval of their vengeful God. While communicating the higher truth of the *core spiritual wound* (perceived separation from God), literal interpretation of this myth has done terrible damage by communicating to us the message that we are unworthy of God's love. As such, we are deprived of the truthful messages about God that help to restore us to our original state of contentment and peace, where we know we are not only loved unconditionally by God, but that we are the very manifestation of love itself.

DEADLY COMPULSION—ENVY

Each of us can relate to the places in our lives where we indulge the fourth core fear *I am not loved*. Falsely perceiving ourselves as separate from God, we have embraced the illusion that love is something outside of us that we are driven to possess. *Envy* is the spiritual compulsion that results out of this unhealed wound. When we experience *envy*, we perceive love as a commodity to be bought and sold. The story of Cain and Abel illustrates this compulsion well.

> *The man had relations with his wife Eve, and she conceived and bore Cain . . . next she bore his brother, Abel. Abel became a keeper of flocks, and Cain a tiller of the soil. In the course of time Cain brought an offering to the Lord from the fruit of the soil, while Abel, for his part, brought one of the best firstlings of his flock. The Lord looked with favor on Abel and his offering, but on Cain and his offering he did not. Cain greatly resented this and was crestfallen. So the Lord said to Cain: "Why are you so resentful and crestfallen? If you do well, you can hold up your head; but if not, sin is a demon lurking at the door; his urge is toward you, yet you can be his master."*
>
> *Cain said to his brother Abel, "Let us go out in the field." When they were in the field, Cain attacked his brother Abel and killed him.*
>
> Genesis 4:1–8

In the story of Cain and Abel, we see that Cain, unaware that he is loved without condition, looks upon God's choice of Abel's offering as a form of favoritism. "God must love Abel more if he chose Abel's gift instead of mine," he reasons. Cain sees God's choice as a rejection not only of his gifts, but of his very self. Cain grows jealous over the favor he perceives God to have bestowed upon his brother. God's choice of Abel's gift illuminates for Cain the wound he carries in his own heart and out of envy, he kills his brother.

We are tempted to believe that the source of love exists outside of us when we forget that our origin is love. From this woundedness, we look outside of ourselves for relationships in which this "love" may be present, and we are driven to possess this "love" and guard it jealously. These counterfeit experiences of "love" reinforce our false belief that we are unworthy of love. In this endless cycle of hope and heartbreak, the love we seek never materializes because we have neglected to heal the *core wound* that caused this false perception in the first place.

The truth about love that we don't want to admit is that no one and nothing outside of us will be ever be able to fill the empty hole we feel inside. The best we can do for each other is to reflect the love we know within ourselves. Jesus affirmed this truth in the following way:

> *You shall love your neighbor as yourself.*
>
> Matthew 22:39

We can only love one another in relation to the love we have accepted within ourselves. This sentiment is not a commandment, but an observed truth that Jesus understood. To some extent, our human relationships will always reflect the degree to which the *core wound* has been healed within us. When we perceive that another is rejecting us, what we are really doing is indulging our own inner rejection of ourselves. When we allow another person's unhealed wound to hurt us, it is only because our own wound is not yet healed. This scenario truly illuminates the challenges we face in our intimate human relationships. Fortunately, our Divine source has equipped our hearts with compassion so that we can face these challenges. Compassion keeps us present to each other through our mutual woundedness so that we may find a pathway for healing. Perhaps it is for this healing that we come together in relationship in the first place.

EASTERN MEDICINE AS A TOOL FOR HEALING— THE HEART CHAKRA

As humans, we have associated this experience of love as somehow connected with our heart space. This is not a coincidence but a deeply intuitive knowledge of the energy center through which love is reflected in our physical, emotional and mental bodies. It is the *heart chakra*, located in the center of our chest that reflects love and the energy of this love that flows through us.

The *heart chakra* reflects the degree to which we believe that we are loved and that we are love itself. Physically, the *heart chakra* is responsible for our circulatory and respiratory systems. As such, it governs our heart and lungs, as well as the transportation of blood and oxygen. The *heart chakra* also governs our immune system through operation of the thymus gland. Additionally, the *heart chakra* corresponds to the state of health of our chest, upper back, arms and hands. Ailments in any of these areas can be an indication that we may be living out of the fear that *we are unworthy of love*. High blood pressure, heart and lung disease, immune system disorders and asthma may be an indication that the wound seeks healing.

Emotionally, when we forget that we are love and suffer the pain of the resulting perceived rejection, we experience the pain of loss along with the feeling of betrayal that can only be described as a broken heart. As a result, we might feel raw, weak, soft, or vulnerable, and our discomfort with these feeling frequently leads us to unhealthy behaviors in an attempt to shield ourselves from this suffering. Resentment, holding grudges and harboring ill thoughts are all behaviors we use to shield ourselves from these moments of perceived rejection. It is these actions that create within us what is frequently referred to as "a hardened heart." Although creating a hardened heart shields us from pain, it also prevents us from feeling the positive feelings of the heart such as love, joy and peace. It is this hardness of heart that God desires to heal in us so that we can once again know the truth of who we are.

I will give them a new heart and put a new spirit within them; I will remove the stony heart from their bodies and replace it with a heart of flesh, so that they will live according to my statutes, and observe and carry out my ordinances; thus they shall be my people and I will be their God.

Ezekiel 11:19

When we allow the healing of our hardened hearts, there is room for the lightness of being to illuminate our experience with peace, joy and love. Simultaneously, we are now vulnerable to the feelings of loss, grief and betrayal. However, staying present to these feelings and allowing grief to freely move through us, we can be healed of loss as well as remain open to the new life promised in the face of this loss. Hardening our hearts only serves to delay the pain that will surface, eventually, in unsavory ways. Pain that is repressed and shielded through a hardened heart, if left untreated, will eventually manifest in physical disease. It is to our advantage to allow God to heal our hardened hearts so that we can not only remember the truth that *we are love*, but reflect that truth for others.

THE RELATIONSHIP BETWEEN BREATH AND LOVE

In the Eastern spiritual and healing traditions, it is said that it is through the breath that we find our place of Oneness with God and with each other. The breath is the pathway to peace, contentment, wisdom, understanding, joy and love. It is for this reason that many Eastern meditation and wellness practices focus on the connection with breath. Zen Meditation, Yoga, Tai Chi and Chi Qong are just a few examples of these types of practices. Centering Prayer in the Christian tradition is another such example. The story of the creation of man illustrates the scriptural awareness of this truth. It is the breath of God, the very love that God is, that gives us life.

> *The Lord God formed man out of the clay of the ground and blew into his nostrils the breath of live, and so man became a living being.*

Genesis 2:7

Conscious awareness of, and attention to, our breath attunes us to this connection with God. When we breathe deeply and mindfully, keeping our thoughts in the present moment, we remember the truth of who we are as One with God in peace, love and joy. When we forget that we are love and live in that place of rejection, we tend to misuse or constrict our breath, thus producing fear, anxiety and restlessness in our bodies. Staying connected with our breath allows us to stand confidently in the knowledge of the love that we are, where we are unaffected by our own or another's perceived rejection.

Integration

Many Eastern meditation practices are rooted in awareness of the breath. You are invited to engage in a practice of mindful breathing. Find a quiet place where you can be undisturbed for 20–30 minutes. Close your eyes and draw your awareness to your breathing. Pay attention to each breath as you draw it in and each breath as you release it. Keep your attention on your breath, and when you feel your mind begin to wander, gently draw it back to awareness of your breath. After engaging in this practice for 20–30 minutes, take a few moments to reflect on how that felt. If there were any thoughts, emotions or sensations that you became aware of record them in your journal.

It is the false perception of separation from God that has caused the *core wound* within us. When this wound remains unhealed within us, one of the ways it manifests is in the fear that *we are not loved*. This fear, *I am not loved*, is then lived out through the compulsion of *envy* that causes us to seek outside ourselves for love. This fear and its corresponding compulsive behaviors then create an imbalance in the *heart chakra* and all the organs to which its energy flows. To help facilitate healing of this fear, we will now explore the sacred truth that not only are *you loved without condition, you are love itself*!

SACRED TRUTH—GOD IS LOVE AND YOU ARE MADE OF THIS LOVE. THIS LOVE CANNOT BE DENIED, NOR DOES IT NEED TO BE EARNED—IT IS YOUR VERY BEING

The deepest desire of the human heart is to be loved: consider the countless fairytales written to illustrate the archetypal truth of this desire and the quest to see this desire fulfilled. We all know the story: the parents (usually the king and queen) reject the young protagonist, who then sets off in search of a handsome prince/ princess who will repair the rejection and restore the love. The archetypal truth expressed here is the woundedness that is common to all of humanity. The rejection experienced by the child, at the hands of one (or both) parents, becomes a metaphor for the *core spiritual wound*. When we perceive ourselves as separate from God, the experience of that separation is most frequently felt as rejection, abandonment and loneliness. This perceived separation from God, which is the Source of love and love itself, obscures the love that is our true nature.

The restoration of our perception of Oneness, so that we can remember the love that we are, is the intention and goal of our human spiritual journey. When we remember our Oneness and live in the truth of that love, we are happy, content, joyful and trusting. We know without a doubt that we are loved because we know the love that we are, and so love is the first and best thing we bring to every experience. We then move through life with a gentleness and ease in the knowledge of this truth. No longer looking for love outside of us we are able to generously give of the love that we are. This generous loving then invites others to remember the love that is their true nature. Providing the tools by which we can live fully in the love that we are is perhaps the greatest gift given to us by the prophets, the mystics and Jesus himself.

There seems to be a direct correlation between our love of self and our belief in God's love. We are more likely to believe that love is our truth when we perceive God as compassionate, loving, gentle and merciful. If we believe God to be punitive, vengeful and judgmental, we tend to judge ourselves harshly and hold ourselves in less than loving regard. As we begin the journey of remembering love as the truth of our identities, it is often helpful to examine and expand our images of God, thereby opening to the truth of God's love.

Happily, wrathful images are not the only representations of God offered in scripture. The greatest of the Hebrew prophets, Jesus of Nazareth and the Christian mystics lay out an entirely different experience of God for us to embrace, one in which God is intimate, personal and deeply loving; one in which God is experienced as a Divine Parent or Lover whose sole desire is for us to return to our awareness of Oneness with God's self. Connecting with this deeply intimate and personal aspect of God is often the first step toward authentic healing of our own inner wounds. As we connect more and more deeply with this aspect of the Divine, we learn the falsehood of separation and move toward embracing the truth of who we are as love. In this awareness, we learn the truth that love is who we are, that is cannot be denied, nor does it have to be earned.

Integration

Read through the scripture passage below. In the place of "O Jacob" and "O Israel", insert your own name. Now, reread the passage as if it is a love letter written directly to you from God. Spend some time reflecting on how this makes you feel. Do you believe that you are precious and glorious and that God loves you? If not, why? Record your reflections in your journal if you feel so called.

> *But now, thus says the Lord, who created you, O Jacob, and formed you, O Israel: Fear not, for I have redeemed you; I have called you by name, you are mine. When you pass through the water, I will be with you; in the rivers you shall not drown. When you walk through fire, you shall not be burned; the flames shall not consume you. For I am the Lord, your God, the Holy One of Israel, your savior. I give Egypt as your ransom, Ethiopia and Seba in return for you. Because you are precious in my eyes and glorious, and because I love you."*
>
> Isaiah 43:1-4a

Contrary to many of the scriptural images of God, Isaiah presents God as passionately and generously loving. Out of love, God created us, calls us, guides and protects us and passionately loves us. How often do we really believe in a God so good? Another deeply passionate image of God comes from the Song of Songs. In this erotic poem, we witness the dialog between God, the Lover and us, the Beloved. This passionate representation of God's desire for us and our desire for God becomes an inspiration for recalling how deeply loved we truly are.

Hark! My lover—here he comes springing across the mountains,
Leaping across the hills.
My lover is like a gazelle or a young stag.
Here he stands behind our wall, gazing through the windows,
*   peering through the lattices.*
My lover speaks; he says to me,
"Arise my beloved, my beautiful one, and come!
For see, the winter is past, the rains are over and gone . . .
Oh my dove in the clefts of the rock, in the secret recesses of
*   the cliff,*
Let me see you, let me hear your voice,
For your voice is sweet, and you are lovely."

Song of Songs 2:8-11, 14

Integration

Spend a few moments composing your own expression of the deepest desire in your heart to know the love of God. Write a poem, a letter, even create a visual representation using crayons, markers or paint. Allow the deepest desires of your heart to find their voice. If you need inspiration for this activity, go online and under images, search for "The Ecstasy of St. Theresa" by Bernini.

In the Judeo-Christian tradition, it is perhaps Jesus of Nazareth who most completely experienced and articulated the deep and intimate love of God. Unlike any teacher before him, Jesus experienced God within the intimacy of the parent-child relationship. God was Jesus' *Abwoon*. While its roots are not gender specific, Abwoon has most commonly been translated as Papa or Father, the more intimate being preferred. This intimate experience and representation of

God was radical to a religious culture that favored the images of God as king, ruler, tyrant and warrior. Jesus' representation of God invites us to remove God from the throne in the clouds, to walk beside us in our human journey, and to allow God not only to walk beside us, but to carry us during those times of need. The story told by Jesus that most effectively communicates this intimate and deeply loving relationship is the story of the prodigal son.

A man had two sons, and the younger son said to his father, "Father, give me the share of your estate that should come to me." So the father divided the property between them. After a few days, the younger son collected all his belongings and set off to a distant country where he squandered his inheritance on a life of dissipation. When he had freely spent everything, a severe famine struck that country, and he found himself in dire need. So he hired himself out to one of the local citizens who sent him to his farm to tend the swine. And he longed to eat his fill of the pods on which the swine fed, but nobody gave him any. Coming to his senses he thought, "How many of my father's hired workers have more than enough food to eat, but here am I, dying from hunger. I shall get up and go to my father and I shall say to him, "Father, I have sinned against heaven and against you. I no longer deserve to be called your son; treat me as you would treat one of your hired workers." So he got up and went back to his father. While he was still a long way off, his father caught sight of him, and was filled with compassion. He ran to his son, embraced him and kissed him. Hi son said to him, "Father, I have sinned against heaven and against you; I no longer deserve to be called your son." But his father ordered his servants, "Quickly bring the finest robe and put it on him; put a ring on his finger and sandals on his feet. Take the fattened calf and slaughter it. Then let us celebrate with a feast, because this son of mine was dead, and has come to life again; he was lost, and has been found." Then the celebration began.

Luke 15:11-24

Integration

You are invited into an experience of Imagination/Contemplation. Read through the story prayerfully. Imagine that you are the younger son. Place yourself in the story and allow the story to unfold for you, imagining every detail. Be aware of any thoughts or emotions that may surface as you experience this story through the eyes of the son. Record your reflections in your journal.

The story of The Prodigal Son is most often used to illustrate the forgiving nature of God. If, like the youngest son, we realize the errors of our ways; ask for forgiveness and change our behaviors, God will forgive us. This interpretation applies conditionality to God's love for us, based solely upon our remorse and act of contrition. Reading this story more carefully, it doesn't seem to be about forgiveness at all, but about God's completely unconditional love. Nowhere in the story does it say that the father was angry or disappointed with the son. Nowhere does it say that the father had rejected the son because of the son's act of independence. Nowhere does the father say, "I forgive you." In fact, he does not even acknowledge as necessary the son's heart-felt confession.

Instead, this is what the story says:

So the son got up and went back to his father. While he was still a long way off, his father caught sight of him, and was filled with compassion. He ran to his son, embraced him and kissed him.

Luke 15:20

While the son was still a long way off, the father caught sight of him. It seems that the father was waiting expectantly for the son's return. Immediately upon seeing his son, the father was filled with compassion. There is no indication in the story that the father was carrying resentment, anger or disgust toward his son. Waiting with arms wide open, the father ran to his son and immediately embraced him.

This is the image of God that Jesus is inviting us to embrace. While God has allowed us, like the younger son, to choose the perception of separation, God waits in anxious anticipation for the moment we decide we have had enough of this pain and suffering. When we consciously choose to remember the love of God and return to an awareness of our Oneness, there is no judgment, no punishment, no anger or resentment. God, filled with compassion, welcomes us with loving arms, embraces and kisses us and orders a great celebration. The need to confess our guilt is ours alone. God loves us without condition and gratefully welcomes us home.

If we can see beyond the fearful images of God, this is the God that we see throughout the Hebrew Scriptures. Our loving God understands our desire to seek independence and the resulting pain of that perceived separation. God knows that the remedy for this pain is to return to our awareness of Oneness with God. This is God's greatest desire for us—to return to the knowledge of the love that we are. It is out of this desire that God gifted to us, through Moses the great covenant. In that covenant agreement with the Israelites, God recognized our on-going struggle with separation and presented to us the remedy for that perceived separation:

Hear O Israel! The Lord is our God, the Lord alone! Therefore, you shall love the Lord, your God, with all your heart, and with all your soul, and with all your strength. Take to heart these words which I enjoin on you today. Drill them into your children. Speak of them at home and abroad, whether you are busy or at rest. Bind them at your wrist as a sign and let them be as a pendent on your forehead. Write them on the doorposts of your houses and on your gates.

Deuteronomy 6:5-9

When we allow ourselves to focus, with all our strength, our hearts, our souls and our minds on God, we move ever more closely to remembering our Oneness with God and the love that is our true nature. This focused attention is the remedy to our human suffering and pain.

In the beginning and middle stages of spiritual growth, it is helpful to perceive God as intimately personal and human-like and as something distinct from us. At the same time, these personal images of God do not begin to touch the vast nature of our Divine Source. Eventually, to truly embrace the fullness of the truth of Oneness, and of love as our true nature, we have to look beyond these personal images to something more infinite. Looking to the deeper translation of the term Abwoon that Jesus so frequently used to address God, we begin to get a glimpse of the vastness of the Divine.

O Thou from whom the breath of life flows and is present in all forms of vibration and light.

(Prayers of the Cosmos, Neil Douglas-Klotz)

It is difficult to grasp the transcendent, indwelling and infinite nature of God with our human mind, and so we have to reach beyond our minds to the lived experience in order to grasp this truth. The writings attributed to John best express the fullness of this lived experience. It is clear through these writings that the author had a deeply personal and experiential relationship with the I Am. It is through this experience that the concept of God as love itself is most clearly articulated.

> *God is love, and whoever remains in love remains in God and God in him. In this is love brought to perfection among us, that we have confidence on the day of judgment because as he is, so are we in this world. There is no fear in love, but perfect love drives out fear because fear has to do with punishment, and so one who fears is not yet perfect in love. We love because God loved us first.*
>
> 1 John 4:16b-19

As the author of John experienced, God is love. Applying this expanded understanding to our existing relationship with God, it stands to reason that if God is love, it is in fact, love that created us. As such, the love that is God lives in and through us. In this way, not only are we loved, we are love itself. Love is, in fact, our rightful inheritance, our true nature, our identity. We are able to live out of this true nature when we remember that we are One with God and hence, one in love.

HOLY VIRTUE—COMPASSION

As we accept the truth that we are One in love with God we become content in the love that we are and we no longer feel compelled to seek that love outside of us. This love-filled contentment invites us to explore the rewriting of our fairytales. As we (the protagonist) come to know the love that is deep within ourselves, we exponentially increase our ability to live in the truth of this love. Knowing that we are comprised of love, we no longer need to build defenses around ourselves, and the fortresses around our hearts begin to disintegrate and we find that we can trust ourselves and others. Understanding that conditional love can never be a source of fulfillment, we no longer find ourselves compelled to seek the handsome prince or beautiful princess that will be able to give us our happily ever after. Love, we remember, is who we are. As we grow in this confidence, we are able to go out into the world reflecting the love that we now know within ourselves. It is here that we shall experience the truest expression of the virtue of *compassion*. It is here that we shall find our happily ever after.

CHAPTER SEVEN

Your Truth Shall Set You Free

"And you will know the truth, and the truth will set you free!"

John 8:32

Truth is often difficult to express. Giving voice to our truth urges us out of our comfort zone into the position of provocation. The truth that God is urging us to reveal frequently flies in the face of societal expectations, norms, traditions and rules. When challenged to express a truth that transcends comfort zones, we become subject not only to our own fears, but also to the fears of anyone else who may be involved. Speaking truth places us in the role of "the grim reaper," appearing out of nowhere to facilitate the change that no one really wants to make—not because the change is unnecessary, but because we are afraid to let go of the known to make way for the new. Jack Nicholson speaks to this truth in the movie *A Few Good Men* when he stated:

"You want the truth? You want the truth? You can't handle the truth!"

The inability—our own or that of others—to handle the truth often silences us and causes us to experience the fifth core fear, the fear that *I am not free to express my truth.*

THE FEAR—I AM NOT FREE TO EXPRESS MY TRUTH

Giving voice to our truth makes us vulnerable. When we indulge our inner prophet, we risk the judgment, criticism and condemnation of others who may be involved. No one likes to be judged, for judgment triggers our own deep-seated fear of rejection. Giving our truth its voice can be dangerous business, but in the end, not giving voice has an even greater cost, for by failing to express our truth, we shall never truly be free.

The story of St. Hildegard of Bingen is one great example of the consequences of withholding our truth. Hildegard of Bingen was a German Abbess who lived in the twelfth century. She was a visionary, mystic, composer, healer, writer, preacher, physician, linguist, counselor, herbalist, philosopher and founder of two monasteries. Forgotten among the countless saints of the Catholic Church, she has been rediscovered through her musical compositions, mystical visions, prolific writing and her system of natural medicine.

From a very early age, Hildegard was gifted with spiritual visions, visions that accompanied her throughout her vowed religious life. She kept these visions to herself, confiding them only to her Spiritual Director, until the year of 1141 when she received a direct call from God commanding her to write down what she saw and what she heard. Hildegard ignored this command out of what she admitted was her own self-doubt and fear of the criticism of others. She soon found herself stricken with an un-diagnosable and seemingly incurable illness that left her bed-ridden. It was only in picking up her pen and writing that she was cured of this mysterious disease.

The story of Hildegard illustrates the potential consequences of denying our truth. In defying the command of God, Hildegard was stricken ill. Was this Divine retribution or the natural consequence of truth denied? Belief in a loving God suggests that it is the latter. When we ignore the truth within us that is seeking its voice, we become choked by the fears that would block us from living and being our most authentic selves. When we deny our gifts and refuse to give voice to God's inspiration, we are denying our very selves. The consequences of this denial will then be reflected in us spiritually, emotionally, mentally and physically.

DEADLY COMPULSION—GREED

God has imparted to us unique and specific gifts through which we are called to reveal God's love, God's peace and God's truth in the world. When we indulge our fears that we lack the ability to express our truth, or that there is something preventing us from doing so, we are suffering from the compulsion of *greed. Greed* comes out of the fear that *we are unable to express our truth* in the world.

We are not alone in the temptation to deny and withhold our gifts. Moses was tempted to believe that his speech impediment would prevent him from communicating God's truth. Jeremiah thought he was too young. Each and every one of us has our own fears and excuses for not openly and freely sharing the gifts that God has given us. Jesus shared this story with his disciples as an example of the consequences of withholding the gifts that God has given us.

THE PARABLE OF THE TALENTS

It will be as when a man who was going on a journey called in his servants and entrusted his possessions to them. To one he gave five talents; to another, two; to a third, one—each according to his ability. Then he went away.

After a long time the master of those servants came back and settled accounts with them. The one who had received five talents came forward bringing the additional five. He said, "Master, you gave me five talents. See, I have made five more."

Then the one who had received two talents also came forward and said, "Master, you gave me two talents. See, I have made two more."

Then the one who had received the one talent came forward and said, "Master, I knew you were a demanding person, harvesting where you did not plant and gathering where you did not scatter; so out of fear I went off and buried your talent in the ground. Here it is back." His master said to him in reply, "You wicked, lazy servant! Throw this useless servant into the darkness outside, where there will be wailing and grinding of teeth."

Matthew 25:14-15, 19-20, 22-23, 24-26a, 30

Integration

Take a few minutes to reflect on your own unique giftedness and how you may or may not be nurturing and sharing this.

Make a list of your own unique gifts and your passions:

- What are the things you LOVE to do?
- What gives you joy?
- What gives you peace?
- How are you currently using these gifts?
- How have you cultivated and nurtured these gifts?
- How are you using these gifts to reveal love, peace and joy in the world?

- What gifts are you not using and why?
- How could you begin to further cultivate these gifts?
- How can you begin to use these gifts to bring peace into our world?

In the parable of the talents, Jesus illustrates the consequence of withholding our gifts from the world. This parable is NOT to be taken literally, but is a metaphor for what happens within us when we fail to nurture and share our gifts. Our inner landscape becomes arid and void of life and we suffer the inner turmoil of the greed that we have chosen to indulge. This story runs parallel to the popular adage, "Use it or lose it." This is the consequence of *greed* indulged.

Since *greed* is typically associated with someone who seeks to acquire great riches, much like the glutton described in chapter three, you may be surprised at the association between greed and the "burying" of our gifts. However, *greed*, when examined from a spiritual perspective goes beyond acquisition to hoarding: it is the miser who hides in his golden castle, acquiring mountains of cash, with no intention of sharing it with anyone but himself. The person who suffers from the spiritual compulsion of *greed* may be fully aware of his or her gifts, but is reluctant or afraid to share them. The spiritually greedy person hides behind their fears, depriving themselves of the freedom that comes from being a vessel of God's love and truth in the world. Unfortunately, when we suffer from *greed*, we hurt more than just ourselves: we deprive the world from experiencing the special way that God's love may be uniquely revealed through us.

Imagine what would have happened if Moses had decided to go back to his tent in the desert, leaving the Israelites to fend for themselves. Or, if instead of heeding the dream to accept Mary into his life, Joseph had exercised his legal right to have her stoned? What if Mary had said no to the angel Gabriel's announcement, refusing to accept God's call to birth Jesus into the world? Our world would be a significantly different place if Moses, Joseph or Mary had refused to give expression to the truth that God had revealed to them. So too is the world lacking when we turn a deaf ear to God's call or when we become mute in the face of the truth God would have us reveal.

There is another face of spiritual *greed* that is often overlooked, but is central to truly authentic freedom—the face of deceit. After all, how can we live authentically if we are indulging in deceit? When the Lord God revealed the law to Moses atop Mount Sinai, included in that law was an admonition against deceit:

> *You shall not bear false witness against your neighbor.*
> Exodus 20:16

We can look at this as an explicit command, which, when broken, will exact God's punishment. Or, as Neale Donald Walsh invites in his series, *Conversation with God*, we can recognize that aligning ourselves in every way with God's truth for us is evidence of our connectedness with God. When we stray from this truth, we have forgotten that place of Oneness with God. In this regard, deceit becomes evidence of the *core wound*—again, that false sense of separation—unhealed. When we lie, we are demonstrating the fears that we have chosen to embrace, rather than the love God would have us know. Deceitful acts spring forth out of the same wound and the same fear that cause us to withhold our gifts from the world. It is in this way that we can understand deceit as a face of *greed*.

Integration

You are invited at this time to participate in a spiritual journaling exercise. Put your pen on the paper and write all your thoughts about expressing truth.

- What truths have you expressed?
- What truths have you withheld?
- When have you given into the temptation to indulge deceit?
- Write down all of your perceived impediments to giving voice to your truth and all the fears that may be standing in your way.

EASTERN MEDICINE AS A TOOL FOR HEALING— THROAT CHAKRA

The *throat chakra*, located in the center of our throat, is the energy center that governs and reflects our ability to listen, hear and give voice to our truth. Where the *sacral chakra* is the center of new life, it is through the *throat chakra* that new life is given its expression. These two centers are intimately connected and we cannot speak of one without giving credit to the other. The seed of new life is energetically planted in the belly and it is through our creative expression—our voice—that this new life is revealed in the world. When we ignore this new life and refuse to allow it to come forth, we suffer and the whole world with us.

Hildegard of Bingen's story clearly illustrates the physical consequence of denying our truth. When we are not expressing our truth, we become spiritually imprisoned and it is not uncommon for this to be reflected in our physical being. The most obvious examples of the physical manifestation of this denial are physical ailments directly related to the *throat chakra*. On a physical level, the *throat chakra* reflects and governs the ears, throat, mouth, teeth, tongue, neck and shoulders. Because of its proximity to the *throat chakra*, the thyroid gland is also included. We can look at the common ailments of the ear and throat for examples of potential manifestations of truths not being spoken: TMJ, ear infections, tinnitus, vertigo, throat cancer, strep throat, chronic neck and shoulder pain, frozen shoulder, hypo- and hyper-thyroid. When we suffer from ailments related to these physical areas, it is often helpful to ask ourselves, "Am I freely and openly expressing my truth?" The next step is to explore any truths that we may not be expressing. Perhaps the root of these ailments is not in the physical, but lies more deeply on the spiritual level, where we are indulging the fear that *we are unable to openly and freely express our truths*, out of the fear of being rejected.

In energy medicine, fibromyalgia, a chronic, debilitating disease that most frequently affects women, is another example of the physical manifestation of truth not being expressed. Western medicine has yet to find a cause, a cure or an effective treatment protocol for this disease that combines debilitating pain with depression. The pain of fibromyalgia often starts in the neck and shoulder area and eventually moves to attack the entire body. It would be interesting to survey those who suffer from this malady to determine if they are freely and openly expressing their truth in the world. The men and women that I know who suffer from this affliction would most decidedly respond, "NO!"

On the emotional and mental levels, there are many ways in which unspoken truth will be made manifest. When we do not feel free to give voice to our truth, it triggers an immediate emotional response. We feel stifled—even choked. Like a wild animal caught in a cage, we become restless, irritated, anxious, panicked and afraid. Anger often becomes the first response as we realize our confinement and struggle to be freed. We may feel insane with the panic of being caught and our desperate desire to be freed. Then, like the animal that realizes its efforts to escape are futile, we sink into despair. We concede to our imprisonment, withdraw to some place within ourselves and become despondent and less alert. We lose our spark, our vitality and our drive to live, for in many ways, we have become dead—dead to our truth—dead to our most authentic self—and we withdraw from the world, seeking shelter within the tomb of our self-deprecating thoughts.

We need only go to the lives of some of our most tortured artists to see this captivity lived out. Sylvia Plath, Virginia Wolfe, Kurt Cobain, Marilyn Monroe, Ernest Hemingway—all extraordinary artists in their own rights, struggling to give voice to the truth that burned within them, only to find themselves haunted by the inner fears that held them captive and eventually drove them to escape. Imagine the amazing jewels we would be able to enjoy if they had been freed of the fears (and mental illnesses) that imprisoned their creative spirits and cut their young lives so very short!

I have seen profound results both within myself and in the lives of clients who have integrated the principles of *authentic freedom* into their existing wellness practices. These principles, along with sound emotional and physical healing practices help to facilitate the freedom that we all so desperately long for. It is in hearing and giving voice to our truth that we can most firmly grasp Jesus' invitation:

"And you will know the truth, and the truth will set you free!"
John 8:3

Integration

I invite you to take a few minutes to reflect on the physical, mental, emotional and spiritual correspondences of the throat chakra.

- What symptoms have you experienced that might be connected with not hearing or giving voice to your truth: Neck and shoulder pain, sore throats, TMJ, ear or throat issues, etc.
- Think of a time when you did not feel free to express your truth. How did you feel?

- Write about a time when you did not feel free to express your truth or when you might have been afraid to share your gifts.

The fear, *I am not free to express my truth* is then the fifth core fear that comes out of the false perception of separation from God. This fear is frequently lived out through the compulsion of *greed* through which we deny or refuse to give voice to God's truth seeking to be expressed through us. Healing this fear leads us more fully into a life of authentic freedom. The key to healing the fear that you are not free to express your truth lies in the sacred truth that it is only in *giving expression to your truth that you will be free.*

SACRED TRUTH—GIVING EXPRESSION TO YOUR TRUTH SHALL SET YOU FREE!

How do we know what is true and what is not? Answering this question seems to be a cause for great confusion in our human journey. There are thousands of books, teachers, preachers, fortune tellers, prophets and self-appointed authorities proclaiming to have a market on the truth and are happy to sell you their version. We need to remember that truth does not lie outside of us, but resides deep within our very being in that place of Oneness with God. The greatest prophets and teachers knew this source of inner knowledge and empowered their disciples to access and embrace this place of truth. Both the prophet Jeremiah and Jesus of Nazareth extended this invitation to the people that grew under their tutelage:

> But this is the covenant which I will make with the house of
> Israel after those days, says the Lord. I will place my law within

them, and write it upon their hearts; I will be their God, and they shall be my people. No longer will they have need to teach their friends and kinsmen how to know the Lord. All, from least to greatest, shall know me, says the Lord.

Jeremiah 31:33–34a

If you love me, you will keep my commandments. And I will ask the Father, and he will give you another Advocate to be with you always, the Spirit of truth, which the world cannot accept, because it neither sees nor knows it. But you know it, because it remains with you and will be in you. I will not leave you orphans; I will come to you. In a little while the world will no longer see me, but you will see me, because I live and you will live. On that day you will realize that I am in my Father and you are in me and I in you.

John 14:15–20

Integration

I invite you to take a few moments to prayerfully reflect on the scripture passages above. Look for a word or phrase that seems to jump out. Spend some time meditating on that word or phrase, asking yourself the question, "What is God saying to me through these words?" Record your reflections in your journal.

Most commonly, these two readings are interpreted to represent some time in the distant future when the kingdom of God will finally be realized. In other words, access to this Divine source of truth will happen in some other time. But, if we understand Jesus' teachings on the kingdom as being present TODAY, then these readings take on a whole new meaning. The Divine Source of truth is present within us . . . RIGHT NOW! If that is true, then why is discerning truth in our lives such a challenge? Jesus responds to this quandary: "On that day you will realize that I am in my Father and you are in me and I in you." What Jesus reminds us is that our perceived separation from God is what stands in the way of our ability to access the Divine source of truth. When we falsely believe ourselves to be separate from God, we cannot connect with the light of truth. When we allow the *core wound* to be healed, then we have more consistent access to not only receiving the message of truth, but to sharing that truth openly in our world. It is in knowing this Oneness with God that we are able to know and give voice to the truth that shall set us free. The source of this truth, as explained by Jeremiah and Jesus is God—and God alone. And when we give voice to this inner authority that is God, then it is the voice of God that speaks through us

Integration

I invite you to take a few minutes to reflect on the role of truth in your own life. Take some time to answer the following questions, recording the responses in your journal if you feel so called.

- What are and have been the sources of external authority in your life?
- How have those sources influenced your own decisions and the path you have take in life?
- Have these sources of authority been positive, negative or a combination thereof?
- How have you connected with the source of authority within?
- Where and when have you heard its voice?

- Have you given it heed, or disregarded that voice? How has this voice been affirmed or silenced?
- Have you given it expression?
- If not, why?
- What is standing in the way of your ability to give voice to your truth?
- How do you know if something is truth or not?
- Where have you experienced the freedom of giving voice to your authentic truth?

Our healing journey is about getting in touch with our most authentic truth and finding ways for that voice to express itself. When we recognize that it is God that is the source of this truth and when we give this truth its expression, we are allowing God to speak in our world. This awareness sheds new light on the importance of this process.

Throughout scripture, we are blessed with stories of men and women who have heard this voice of truth and given it voice. In allowing themselves to be vessels through which God's truth is revealed in the world, they have come to know the freedom of Oneness with God. The call of Samuel is one such example:

During the time young Samuel was minister to the Lord under Eli, a revelation of the Lord was uncommon and vision infrequent. One day Eli was asleep in his usual place. His eyes had lately grown so weak that he could not see. The lamp of God was not yet extinguished and Samuel was sleeping in the temple of the Lord where the ark of God was. The Lord called to Samuel, who answered, "Here I am." He ran to Eli and said, "Here I am, you called me." "I did not call you," Eli said, "go back to sleep." So Samuel went back to sleep. Again the Lord called Samuel, who rose and went to Eli. "Here I am," he said, "You called me." But he answered, "I did not call you, my son. Go back to sleep."

At that time, Samuel was not familiar with the Lord, because the Lord had not revealed anything to him as yet. The Lord called Samuel again, for the third time. Getting up and going to Eli, he said, "Here I am. You called me." Then Eli understood that the Lord was calling the youth. So he said to Samuel, "Go to sleep, and if you are called, reply, 'Speak, Lord, for your servant is listening.'" When Samuel went to sleep in his place, the Lord came and revealed his presence, calling out as before, "Samuel, Samuel!" Samuel answered, "Speak, for your servant is listening."

Integration

You are invited to participate in an exercise of Imagination/Contemplation, using the scripture passage above. Read through the passage slowly and prayerfully. Choose a character, Samuel, Eli, God, or some unnamed witness. Through your imagination, enter fully into the scene, imagining the surroundings, what you are wearing, the temperature, smells, etc. Allow the scene to unfold in your mind. Then, moving through the narrative, imagine the events as they are unfolding from the perspective of the character you have chosen. Have fun and let your imagination run wild. After you have completed the story, record what happened in your journal. Pay special attention to any thoughts, emotions or reactions that surfaced. Then, go back and read your journal entry. How is God speaking to you through what was revealed?

In the story of Samuel, we have an example of a young man who has not yet discovered the voice of truth that spoke within him. Prior to his encounter with God, he had planned his life based on the direction of those outside of himself. Hearing God's voice for the first time, Samuel discovers, with the help of his wise teacher Eli, a new source of authority. God will now be the source that will direct his life. In accepting this inner source of truth, Samuel is free to embrace his life purpose. No longer will he be the servant of Eli, he will become a vessel through which God's voice will be revealed to Israel. Samuel, willingly and freely accepts the call God has given him and discovers the freedom of this newfound place of Oneness with God.

Samuel is not unique in the call to being a vessel through which God's truth may be revealed in our world. Each and every one of us is uniquely called to be channels for this truth. We discussed in Chapter Four the unique giftedness that each of us possesses. Samuel's was the gift of prophecy. Yours may be the gift of healing, preaching, teaching, discernment, understanding, wisdom, etc., etc., etc. God alone can reveal to you the unique gifts that you have been given to help to bring about the fullness of God's kingdom. Fortunately, there are a million different ways in which God reveals truth to us. We simply need to take the time to listen, be open to believing the truth as it is revealed, and then have the courage to give it its voice. But where are we to look for the voice of God in our lives?

LISTENING AND HEARING OUR TRUTH

If we turn again to scripture, we see a multitude of examples of God revealing truth. Samuel heard the voice of God waking him out of his sleep. Moses experienced God through the burning bush. The Israelites, while on their journey through the desert, saw God in a column of smoke and a pillar of fire. Adam and Eve, Noah, Jacob,

Joseph, Miriam the Prophetess, Jeremiah, Isaiah, Job, Mary—the Mother of Jesus, Elizabeth—the mother of John the Baptist, Anna the Prophetess—the list goes on and one. Of course, we do not want to omit Jesus, himself. Each and every one of these people listened, heard and gave heed to the word of God that was revealed to them. Although God was revealed to each of these individuals in a special and unique way, there is a common process that was followed by each of these truth bearers that we too are invited to embrace.

Of all the characters in scripture, Jesus offers the most powerful example of the first step in this process of hearing and giving voice to God's truth. The driving force of Jesus' ministry was his personal relationship with God, and he frequently, in fact always, took time to cultivate and nurture that relationship.

> *"The report about him spread all the more, and great crowds assembled to listen to him and to be cured of their ailments, but he would withdraw to deserted places to pray."*
>
> Luke 5:15-16

Not only did he cultivate that relationship for himself, he taught his disciples to do the same:

> *"When you pray, do not by like the hypocrites, who love to stand and pray in the synagogues and on street corners so that others may see them. Amen, I say to you, they have received their reward. But when you pray, go to your inner room, close the door, and pray to the Father in secret. Your Father who sees in secret will repay you. In praying, do not babble like the pagans, who think that they will be heard because of their many words. Do no be like them. Your Father knows what you need before you ask him."*
>
> Matthew 6:5-8

Integration

Take a few minutes to prayerfully read the scripture passage from Matthew on page 114. Contemplate on your own prayer life. Take time to reflect on the following questions, recording your responses in your journal if you feel so called.

- In what ways have you been cultivating your relationship with God?
- What is your current understanding of prayer and how do you pray?
- Where are you taking time to listen for God's voice in your life?
- What is your "inner room" and how have you cultivated that?

In Jesus' instruction on prayer, he seems to be saying that it is not the words that are important, but the ability to be present to God in our "inner room"—that place of silence within—where we can connect with God in secret, knowing the intimacy and depth of God's love. It is here that God's truth shall be revealed. Recitation of rote, memorized prayers, without an opportunity for active silence, does not leave us open to listening and hearing the voice of God in our lives.

In his book, *Setting a Trap for God*, Rocco Errico reminds us of the Aramaic concept of prayer. Prayer, he explains is really a form of "attunement"—it is the way in which we adjust our personal frequencies to match that of God's so that we can receive God's message. He likens it to a radio tuner, changing the channel until we have a clear connection with God's channel. This is a lovely metaphor for what we are doing when we set time aside to pray.

Not only are we connecting with the Source of truth that is God, but in the process, we are being healed as our personal frequency more closely resonates with that of God's. The more frequently we tend to this task of "attunement", the more fully we are drawn into the knowledge of God's love. In this way, prayer becomes the most powerful of tools.

Integration

I would invite you at this time, or at a time in the near future, to set aside time to go to your inner room and pray to God in secret. Take 10–15 minutes to simply rest in silence. Allow your intention to simply be to listen. Listen to the world around you; listen to your breath; listen to the sound of your heartbeat. Allow these activities of listening to draw you deeper within to a place you may not yet know—that deep place of silence within. Practice this activity everyday for a week, and pay attention to the slowing down and quieting that is taking place within. Have no attachment to what this experience should look like. There is no goal, but to practice being quiet and listening.

Silence is a remarkable way to connect with the profound peace and truth of God. However, for those of us who wrestle unceasingly to find that place of silence, it is a relief to know that God is not only revealed in the silence, but is also revealed in the cacophony of our daily lives. God is present in the noise, too. In fact, one of my favorite stories in scripture is a story in which truth is revealed to Jesus in the most unexpected way—a truth that forever changed the course of his ministry:

Then Jesus went from that place and withdrew to the region of Tyre and Sidon. And behold, a Canaanite woman of that district came and called out, "Have pity on me, Lord, Son of David! My daughter is tormented by a demon." But he did not say a word in answer to her. His disciples came and asked him, "Send her away, for she keeps calling out after us." He said in reply, "I was sent only to the lost sheep of the house of Israel." But the woman came and did him homage, saying, "Lord, help me." He said in reply, "It is not right to take the food of the children and throw it to the dogs." She said, "Please, Lord, for even the dogs eat the scraps that fall from the table of their masters." Then Jesus said to her in reply, "O woman, great is your faith! Let it be done for you as you wish." And her daughter was healed from that hour.

Matthew 15:21-28

In this story, Jesus hears the voice of God through the pleas of the Canaanite woman. Prior to this encounter, Jesus believed his ministry to be limited to "the lost sheep of Israel." Through the passionate pleas of the Canaanite woman, Jesus hears another truth: he awakens from *his* prejudice to the realization that perhaps his ministry is not limited to the Jews, but is for the benefit of all humankind. The encounter with the Canaanite woman marked a dramatic transition in Jesus' ministry and opened the doors to the universal intent of his mission. As Paul said in his letter to the Galatians:

There is neither Jew nor Greek, there is neither slave nor free person, there is not male and female; for you are all one in Christ Jesus.

Galatians 3:28

In this story, the Canaanite woman served as the voice of God for Jesus. Through her persistence, Jesus became aware of the fullness of his mission. So too, in our own lives, there are messengers sent to wake us up, to be the voice of God that shakes us from our stagnation and personal bias, to get us off of the path of our own egos and return us to the path that God has in store for us—a path that is far greater than the one we would create on our own.

Integration

This exercise is inspired by a similar exercise in the book *Love* from the *Take and Receive* series by Sr. Marie Schwan and Jaclyn Syrup-Bergin. On a page in your journal, make a timeline, beginning with the day you were born up until today. On the time line, mark the significant events of your life—positive and negative—anything you consider to be significant to who and where you are today. Take time to reflect on each of those events, opening your awareness to how God was present to you through that experience. Look for how God spoke to you or is now speaking to you through that experience. Record your reflections in your journal.

In this exercise you began the process of incorporating the practice of *active contemplation* into your everyday life. Through active contemplation we move out of the silence into the vibrant movement of our lives. In this form of prayer, we ask God to open your ears and eyes to how God is present in EVERY moment of your life. We begin to look at every moment of our lives as a way to become aware of the presence and action of God. We begin by paying attention to the routine actions of our lives—eating, sleeping, working, playing and reflecting in the midst of these activities on how God is being revealed. We pay attention to our surroundings, nature, animals, the weather and ask how God is being revealed. We explore the presence of God in our personal relationships, the people we encounter, those little "coincidences" that seem to make a difference. Active contemplation opens us up to the awareness of God's intimate attention to our lives. Every moment becomes an opportunity to experience, see and hear the truth of God. This then becomes another way to listen and hear the truth that God would reveal along each place in our journeys.

Now that we have explored some of the ways that we can take time to listen and hear God's truth in our lives, we need to move on to the final step: Speaking our truth. It is said that our greatest fear as human beings is to speak in public. In fact, this fear ranks higher even than our fear of death. We would rather die than speak in public! That is a significant statement! The challenge of speaking our truth is not unlike the challenge of speaking in public—the thought of it is simply terrifying! When we speak our truth, we are putting ourselves out there and subjecting ourselves to the judgment and criticism of others. This is not a comfortable position to be in, and yet it is only in giving voice to our truth that we can ever hope to be truly free. Jesus speaks to this in the following reading from Matthew:

> *You are the salt of the earth. But if the salt loses its taste, with what can it be seasoned? It is no longer good for anything but to be thrown out and trampled underfoot. You are the light of the world. A city set on a mountain cannot be hidden. Nor do they light a lamp and then put it under a bushel basket; it is set on a lampstand, where it gives light to all in the house. Just so, your light must shine before other, that they may see your good deeds and glorify your heavenly Father.*
>
> Matthew 5:13–16

Integration

Take a few minutes to prayerfully read the scripture passage on page 119. You are then invited to use the following phrases as a *mantra prayer*, silently repeating the phrases over and over in your mind with an awareness that theses phrases pertain to you directly. As you repeat the phrases, observe how they are allowing you to enter into a peaceful, meditative state. Continue repeating the phrases. Pay attention to any thoughts, phrases, emotions or reflections that arise as you enter into the depths of these phrases. Record your reflection in your journal if you feel so called. These are the phrases to be used as a mantra:

> *I am the salt of the earth*
> *I am the light of the world*

As we discussed in chapter 4, each and every one of us has been uniquely gifted to be vessels through which God's reign of peace can be made manifest in our world. We are each called to "be the body of Christ." This is what Jesus is reminding us of in this reading from Matthew's gospel. Not only are we uniquely gifted, this giftedness carries with it a profound responsibility. We are not called to conceal these gifts or reserve them solely for our own use. No, we are commissioned by God to freely and openly share these gifts in the world. It is only through the unfettered sharing of these gifts that God's desire can be made complete. This is an incredible responsibility, but much more than that, it is an incredible gift. Just think: YOU play a role in the peace and love of God being made manifest in our world!

Saying yes to this call is not easy. It requires that we listen and carefully discern the truth that God would reveal to us. More difficult still, once we have discerned the truth and the unique way we are being called to reveal this truth, we have to give it a voice. Expressing the truth that God has revealed to us through our own unique giftedness is perhaps the most difficult part of this process. We need only look at the men and women of scripture to realize how truly difficult this task is of speaking our truth—Moses who claimed he was not eloquent of speech (Exodus 4:10, 13), Jeremiah who was too young (Jeremiah 1:4-6), Jesus who thought he only came for the lost children of Israel (Matthew 15:23b-24). As each of these examples illustrate, none of these perceived impediments can stand in the way of God working through us. In fact, it is often through our greatest weakness that God is most profoundly revealed.

> *Indeed, the parts of the body that seem to be weaker are all the more necessary, and those parts of the body that we consider less honorable we surround with greater honor . . .*
>
> 1 Corinthians 12:22-23b

Integration

Take a few minutes to reflect on weakness as a gift. Take some time to reflect and write your reflections on the questions below:

- What do you perceive to be your weaknesses?
- How have your perceived weaknesses placed you in a position of receiving love, charity, support, mercy?
- How have your perceived weaknesses allowed others to share their gifts?
- How have your perceived weaknesses invited humility and an awareness of your own powerlessness in the face of God?

- How have you been able to serve others through your perceived weaknesses, allowing you to be "the wounded healer?"

Giving full expression to our truth includes being vulnerable enough to allow our perceived weaknesses to be out in the open. When Christopher Reeve, my generation's Superman, became paralyzed as a result of a polo accident, he could have chosen the life of a recluse. Instead, he used his celebrity, working tirelessly, in the public eye, for spinal chord research. There are countless stories of survival through which people have used their perceived weaknesses to create transformation and positive change in our world. The same is true for you. What you perceive to be a weakness may indeed prove to be your greatest strength.

HOLY VIRTUE—GENEROSITY

> *You are the salt of the earth. But if the salt loses its taste, with what can it be seasoned? It is no longer good for anything but to be thrown out and trampled underfoot. You are the light of the world. A city set on a mountain cannot be hidden. Nor do they light a lamp and then put it under a bushel basket; it is set on a lampstand, where it gives light to all in the house. Just so, your light must shine before other, that they may see your good deeds and glorify your heavenly Father.*
>
> Matthew 5:13-16

The gifts that we are given by God, through which we are invited to reveal God's presence in the world, are not to be hidden but are to be shared freely and openly. As we learn to let go of the fear that *I am not free to express my truth* and work toward embracing the truth that *the truth shall set us free*, we find ourselves freely and openly sharing our gifts. No longer encumbered by the false perception of separation, we generously share our truth in the world. *Generosity* is the virtue by which we can measure the degree to which we have embraced the truth of Oneness with God and with each other. As we generously share our most authentic selves, we experience the liberation of a life of God's deepest desire for us.

CHAPTER EIGHT

The Source of Knowledge Is Within

I will place my law within them, and write it upon their hearts; I will be their God and they shall be my people. No longer will they have need to teach their friends and kinsmen how to know the Lord. All from least to greatest shall know me, says the Lord.

Jeremiah 31:33–34

THE FEAR—I DO NOT KNOW

The core spiritual fear, *I do not know* is rooted in the false perception that we do not or cannot know the truth. As is the case with all the *core fears*, the source of this fear flows from our perceived separation from God, for if we are separate from God, how can we know God's truth? This fear, rooted within our own woundedness, is reinforced by parents, teachers, ministers, government leaders, etc., who unknowingly teach and perpetuate the myth that *we do not or cannot know the truth*. Then, we too carry this fear out into the world, spreading it like a virus so that ultimately, it controls the very structures and policies of our social organizations, including those of our government.

The fear that *we do not or cannot know our truth* is compounded when parents, teachers, ministers, government leaders and other perceived authorities proclaim to have a monopoly on the truth, thereby squelching our desire or ability to even try to seek it out for ourselves. By taking the path of least resistance and blindly accepting someone else's truth we are shocked to discover that what may be truth for one may not be truth for all.

What we have forgotten is that there is only one absolute truth and that is God.

Integration

I invite you to take a few minutes to reflect on the fear *I do not or cannot know the truth* and how you may be experiencing it in your own life.

- Where do you fear that you do not have the gifts, experience, knowledge or intelligence to know the truth?
- Where do you doubt or feel confused about the truth that God seems to be revealing to you?
- Where have you had moments of insight, intuition, physical or spiritual vision or dreams that seem to be revealing truth to you?
- How did you respond in those moments?
- What are the messages you received as a child that either supported or denied your ability to receive and believe in the truth that God would reveal to you?

❧

DEADLY COMPULSION—SLOTH

When we falsely perceive ourselves as separate from God and experience the sixth core fear that *I do not or cannot know the truth*, we live out that fear through the compulsion of *sloth*. Webster's dictionary defines sloth as: "disinclination to action or labor." In a physical sense, we think of this as laziness. It could also be taken to imply a refusal to accept responsibility for ones actions, thoughts or behaviors. In a spiritual sense, it is the latter which is especially true, with the added aspect of refusing to accept, use and take responsibility for the gifts that we have been given by God to reason, discern and exercise truth. When we indulge the compulsion of *sloth* in this more spiritual sense, we have forgotten the source of truth within in our connection with God, and have surrendered to the fear that *I do not or cannot know the truth*. The following story of The Man Born Blind illustrates this kind of *sloth*.

> As Jesus walked along, he saw a man blind from birth. His disciples asked him, "Rabbi, who sinned, this man or his parents, that he was born blind?" Jesus answered, "Neither this man nor his parents sinned; he was born blind so that God's works might be revealed in him.
>
> When Jesus had said this, he spat on the ground and made mud with the saliva and spread the mud on the man's eyes, saying to him, "Go, wash in the pool of Siloam" (which means Sent). Then he went and washed and came back able to see.
>
> They brought to the Pharisees the man who had formerly been blind. Now it was a Sabbath day when Jesus made the mud and opened his eyes. Then the Pharisees also began to ask him how he had received his sight. Some of the Pharisees said, "This man is not from God, for he does not observe the Sabbath." But others said, "How can a man who is a sinner perform such signs?" And they were divided.

So for the second time, they called the man who had been blind, and they said to him, "Give Glory to God! We know that this man is a sinner." He answered, "I do not know whether he is a sinner. One thing I do know, that though I was blind, now I see." They answered him, "You were born entirely in sin, and are you trying to teach us?" And they drove him out.

Jesus said, "I came into this world for judgment so that those who do not see may see, and those who do see may become blind." Some of the Pharisees near Jesus heard this and said to him, "Surely we are not blind, are we?" Jesus said to them, "If you were blind, you would not have sin. But now that you say, 'We see', your sin remains."

John 9:1-3, 6-7, 13-15, 16, 24-25, 34, 39-41

Integration

You are invited to enter into an exercise of Imagination/Contemplation, using the story of "The Man Born Blind." Read the scripture passage above (or for the text in its entirety, go to John 9:1-41) slowly and prayerfully, looking for a character that jumps out at you—Jesus, one of the disciples, the blind man, the Pharisees or an unnamed bystander. Go back and reread the passage viewing it from the perspective of your chosen character. After rereading the passage, enter into your own imagination, allowing the story to unfold from the perspective of your character; Imagine every detail—what you are wearing, the people around you, the physical surroundings, the weather, etc. Allow your imagination to run wild as the story unfolds in your mind. Pay attention to any emotions you may experience, or thoughts that may emerge. Record your reflection in your journal, allowing additional details to emerge. After writing your story, go back and read your own story and reflect on how this may be reflective of where you are in your own spiritual journey. What might God be revealing to you through this exercise of Imagination/Contemplation?

The story of the Man Born Blind illustrates the compulsion of *sloth* and the healing way in which God reveals truth to us. In this story, the man is depicted as being physically blind. The disciples ask Jesus a practical question regarding this depiction based on the theology in which they were raised. Hebrew doctrine at the time held that if someone was born with a physical deformity or handicap, it was punishment for either the sins of the parents, or their own sin. Jesus begins to reveal truth to the disciples by turning this belief on its tail: *"Neither he nor his parents sinned; it is so that the works of God might be made visible through him."* Jesus opens the eyes of his disciples to the truth, revealing the illusion of their formerly held belief. To the disciples, this created an earth-shattering shift. As we read on in the story, it becomes apparent that not everyone was readily able to embrace this truth, nor were they able to accept the works of God that were made visible through the Man Born Blind.

What we see in this story is the conflict between commonly held beliefs and the truth that God might reveal. In the story, Jesus cures the man of his physical blindness. This is a good thing, right? Not from the perspective of the Pharisees. The Pharisees encompassed a specific sect within the Hebrew tradition. They were strict adherents of the law and believed it was only through the law that God's approval could be gained. Anyone living outside the law was considered to be a "sinner" and therefore, unworthy of God. As such, the fact that Jesus cured this man on the Sabbath, immediately put Jesus' state of worthiness into question. *"This man is not from God, because he does not keep the Sabbath."* The law states the healing on the Sabbath is forbidden, therefore from the perspective of the Pharisees, Jesus could not be from God. But if Jesus is not from God, how is it that he was able to heal? It was this question that the Pharisees, along with the other witnesses, struggled to comprehend. Very few were able to openly accept the reality of the healing or that it was God that facilitated this healing through Jesus. The man who had been born blind was healed, while those who could see chose to remain in darkness. The Pharisees and those who sided with them suffered from the compulsion of *sloth* when they chose to see through the lens of their closely-held perceptions and in their narrow-mindedness refused to see the truth right before their eyes. The Pharisees held so tightly to what they believed as truth (the law), that they were unable to accept the truth that was revealed before them. Blinded by the power they had received through the law (as designated interpreters and enforcers of the law), they were unable to be open to the possibility that God might work beyond their own limited point of view.

Unfortunately, the Pharisees were not alone in entertaining the compulsion of *sloth* on that day. What of all the bystanders who witnessed this miracle and still questioned if Jesus was from God? What of the man's own parents who refused to answer the questions put to them by the Judeans for fear of being put out of the temple? What about the disciples themselves who immediately judged the blind man on the basis of sinfulness? All of these were openly exhibiting the compulsion of *sloth*.

Like the Pharisees and the bystanders in the story of the Man Born Blind, we too suffer from the compulsion of *sloth*. *Sloth* is lived out in our society in many forms. We are guilty of *sloth* when we fail to exercise the gifts that God gave us to reason, and to discern truth. *Sloth* allows us to avoid taking responsibility for our lives. We no longer have to take the time to allow God's truth to be revealed. Instead we rely on so-called experts to tell us what to do. *Sloth* allows us to remain in the perceived safety of "status quo," going along with what is socially acceptable or agreed upon by our chosen circle of influence. The source of direction, guidance and law becomes an external perceived authority rather than the internal, authentic source of truth, which is God. In this model, we blindly follow the perceived authority, never testing to see if the guidance is truly of God.

Sloth lived out on a collective basis becomes tyranny. Ignorance, slavery, prejudice, racism, sexism and terrorism are all examples of what happens when we fail to exercise our responsibility to discern truth. This collective inaction allows the perceived authority to maintain power and control over the masses, commanding policies, decisions and actions without question or challenge. When we fail to exercise discernment and hold authority accountable, our civil liberties and freedoms are slowly stripped away. When we turn a blind eye to this abuse of power, it only becomes stronger. We need only look to Nazi Germany for an example of the dangers of this kind of collective *sloth*.

Integration

Take a few minutes to reflect on the spiritual understanding of *sloth*:

- What are your thoughts and reflections about this new understanding? Where might you be experiencing sloth in your own life?
- Where have you found yourself deferring to an external "authority" for guidance, rules or direction, rather than going within to access God's truth for you. Why?
- What is the cause of sloth in your own life and how might you invite God to heal you from this compulsion?
- Where do you experience sloth as being exercised in society?

- Where are the situations in which you have witnessed individuals giving up their own truth for that of an outside authority?
- Where have you witnessed perceived authorities who claim to hold a monopoly on truth?
- What are the consequences of this for both the individual and for society as a whole?
- Where have you doubted the truth that God has revealed to you and why?

EASTERN MEDICINE AS A TOOL FOR HEALING— THE BROW CHAKRA

As we seek to know truth in our lives, we are supported by the energy system that moves in and through us. It is through the sixth chakra—the *brow chakra*, that we are One with the mind of God and it is through this energy center that God's truth is revealed. When we are open to receiving and believing this truth the *brow chakra* remains in a state of balance. When we are closed to receiving or believing that truth, the *brow chakra* is in a state of disease.

The *brow chakra* is located in the center of our foreheads, just between our eyebrows. On a physical level, the *brow chakra* governs our physical sight. When the *brow chakra* is balanced, our physical vision is clear, sharp and free of disease. Diseases of the eye or disturbances in our vision can be indicators of the *brow chakra* in a state of imbalance. On a mental level the *brow chakra* governs our ability to acquire, retain and retrieve knowledge. It is the energy center that governs our learning, comprehension, understanding and memory. Emotionally, a balanced *brow chakra* supports a clear mind that is sharp and free of confusion. Spiritually, the *brow chakra* governs our ability to receive, discern, believe and embrace Divine truth.

The *brow chakra* is intimately connected with what Eastern Mystics have come to know as *the third eye*. The third eye is the eye through which we see through the eyes and the mind of God. It is here that we are one with the mind of God and able to receive God's truth, knowledge, understanding, vision and insight. It is in cultivating this connection that we are able to know the truth that comes from God, rather than the illusions we create through our egos. When this connection is nurtured and maintained we can be open to knowing the truth of God and are able to maintain an attitude of humility, recognizing that the only true source of truth is God.

The *brow chakra* and the organs to which this energy flows are negatively impacted by the fear that *I do not or cannot know the truth* and its resulting compulsion of *sloth*. The key to healing this fear is to remember that the source of truth is God and that we are One with this Source.

SACRED TRUTH—ALL WISDOM, KNOWLEDGE AND TRUTH ARE AVAILABLE TO YOU THROUGH GOD

How is it that we can know God's truth in our lives? How do we know which direction to take, which path to choose? Life would be a whole lot easier if God were to simply drop a brick on our heads or paste our truth on the nearest billboard. We all yearn to experience the flashing sign, angelic encounter or star in the sky that will direct us toward our truth. We yearn to know who we are, how to more fully understand God and to know what our unique contribution may be in the world. This longing is echoed by the Psalmist:

Make known to me your ways, Lord;
Teach me your paths.
Guide me in your truth and teach me,
For you are God my savior.

Psalm 25:4-5

We all yearn to know God's truth, but unfortunately, encounters with flying bricks or flashing signs are rare. Instead, we haphazardly throw noodles against the wall, hoping something will stick. The challenge is that most of us are not aware that we have the tools through which we can be empowered to receive and discern the truth that God reveals. In many cases, we have been discouraged (or even forbidden) from believing that Divine revelation is possible, or we have been told to ignore or doubt the voice or vision of truth as it tries to find its expression through us. Afraid of being labeled as crazy or delusional, we often suppress this truth, ignoring the Divine/human communication that is as natural and as much a part of our human experience as the very act of breathing.

Integration

Take a few minutes to reflect on your own process of seeking truth in your life:

- Where have you sought to know truth in your life?
- What are the tools that you use to be open to receiving truth?
- What are the signs that you have experienced that have led you in your journey of truth?
- Reflect on how the following things have been markers of truth in your journey: intuition, imagination, knowledge, learning, coincidences, signs and omens, personal relationships, dreams.

❧

In the last chapter, we explored the ways in which God reveals truth to us through our "listening" and "hearing" and how we are called to give that truth its voice. In this chapter, we will focus on the other vehicles that God uses to reveal truth. Specifically, we will focus on the ways in which truth is revealed through our eyes and our mind, recognizing that *we are one with the mind of God and it is here that truth is revealed*. In the end, we will discover that truth is actually easy to find, we just have to see and have the strength to believe.

> *I will place my law within them, and write it upon their hearts;*
> *I will be their God and they shall be my people. No longer*
> *will they have need to teach their friends and kinsmen how to*
> *know the Lord. All from least to greatest shall know me, says*
> *the Lord.*
>
> Jeremiah 31:33–34

In this reading from Jeremiah, we begin to get a glimpse into our intimate connection with God's truth, *"I will place my law within them, and write it upon their hearts."* Not unlike Jesus' proclamation of the kingdom, this reading is often misunderstood to represent an occurrence that will happen in some distant future. Instead, we are invited to recognize that God's truth (the law) is already planted within us and written upon our hearts. We are not separate from God's truth, it cannot be taken away from us and we do not have to earn it. More importantly, this reading tells us that this is God's greatest desire—that we know this intimate connection with truth. Why then, is accessing this truth often such a struggle?

The challenge to knowing truth, in many cases, is that we have been told we can't. We don't have the proper education; haven't lived a holy enough life; haven't made the appropriate sacrifices; aren't of the right gender, religion, social standing, race, etc., etc., etc. As damaging as these messages can be, even more detrimental are the times we have connected with truth and been told we were wrong, or that our gifts of seeing and knowing were "Not of God." These messages invalidate us, causing us to doubt the truth that we do know, and prevent us from cultivating our connection with the source of truth. It is easy to cast blame on the outside influences that have served to undermine our connection with truth. In the end, however, the true source of this struggle is our own false perception of separation from God. It is this unhealed wound that prevents us from being able to freely and consistently access and believe the truth that God would reveal. It is the unhealed *core wound* in us that leaves us vulnerable to the unhealed *core wound* in another, causing us to believe the self-proclaimed truth of an external "perceived authority" over the inner true Source of authority. The answer is to seek healing of the *core wound* so that we may once again recognize and believe the truth of God that is written in our hearts.

When we are able to remember our Oneness with God, we are able to freely and openly receive, believe and embrace the truth that God would reveal to us and remain free of the illusions of our own and the collective ego. Living in God's truth allows us to experience the spiritual freedom that God intended, where we persistently and consistently know peace. Fortunately, Hebrew and Christian scripture supports the fact that this Divine revelation is not only possible, but is one of God's greatest desires.

Make known to me your ways, Lord; teach me your paths.
Guide me in your truth and teach me, for you are God my
savior.
Good and upright is the Lord, who shows sinners the way,
Guides the humble rightly and teaches the humble the way.
All the paths of the Lord are faithful love
toward those who honor the covenant demands.
Who are those who fear (are in awe of) the Lord?
God shows them the way to choose.

The counsel of the Lord belongs to the faithful; the covenant instructs them.

My eyes are ever upon the Lord, who frees my feet from the snare.

Psalms 25:4–5; 8–10; 12; 14–15

"And you will know the truth, and the truth will set you free!"

John 8:32

The Advocate, the Holy Spirit that the Father will send in my name—he will teach you everything and remind you of all that I told you. Peace I leave with you; my peace I give to you. Do not let your hearts be troubled or afraid.

John 14:26–27

I have much more to tell you, but you cannot bear it now. But when he comes, the Spirit of truth, he will guide you to all truth. He will not speak on his own, but he will speak what he hears, and will declare to you the things that are coming.

John 16:12–13

In each of these passages, we see that God readily reveals truth to us, and that God's desire is that we be open to receiving and believing this truth. And, when you think about it, is there anything (even within ourselves) that could block God's communication with us? Of course not! Just as God's love for us and desire for us to know the truth is infinite, so are the number of ways for God to reveal truth to us. History abounds with fascinating examples of God's methods, including physical and spiritual visions, dreams, intuition, wisdom and life experiences. Our role is to be open, and then to carefully discern whether or not what we perceive as truth is coming from God or our own ego. What follows are a few illustrations of some of the ways that God reveals truth to us through our physical and spiritual vision, dreams, intuition, wisdom and our life experiences.

PHYSICAL VISION

A long time passed, during which the king of Egypt died. Still the Israelites groaned and cried out because of their slavery. As their cry for release went up to God, he heard their groaning and was mindful of his covenant with Abraham, Isaac and Jacob. He saw the Israelites and knew . . .

Meanwhile, Moses was tending the flock of his father-in-law Jethro, the priest of Midian. Leading the flock across the desert, he came to Horeb, the mountain of God. There an angel of the Lord appeared to him in fire flaming out of a bush. As he looked on, he was surprised to see that the bush, though on fire, was not consumed. So Moses decided, "I must go over to look at this remarkable sight, and see why the bush is not burned."

When the Lord saw him coming over to look at it more closely, God called out to him from the bush, "Moses! Moses!" He answered, "Here I am." God said, "Come no nearer! Remove the sandals from your feet, for the place where you stand is holy ground. I am the God of your father," he continued, "the God of Abraham, the God of Isaac, the God of Jacob." Moses hid his face, for he was afraid to look at God. But the Lord said, "I have witnessed the affliction of my people in Egypt and have heard their cry of complaint against their slave drivers, so I know well what they are suffering. Therefore, I have come down (initiated an extraordinary Divine intervention) to rescue them from the hands of the Egyptians and lead them out of that land into a good and spacious land, a land flowing with milk and honey . . . Come now! I will send you to Pharaoh to lead my people, the Israelites out of Egypt."

Exodus 3:1–10

Integration

You are invited to enter into an exercise of mindfulness, where you seek God's presence in the seemingly ordinary characteristics of an orange. Eat this orange as if you had never before eaten an orange, or even seen an orange in your life. Take some time to really examine the orange—its color, texture, weight, smell, etc. Really focus on this orange, inviting God into the experience to see how God is expressing God's self through the created object of an orange. Reflect on the nature and purpose of an orange. How are oranges used? When you are ready to eat the orange, peel it slowly, gently, paying attention to each action of peeling the orange. What do you notice; does anything happen that you hadn't noticed other times when you have eaten an orange? Then slowly, and meditatively, eat the orange, section by section. Savor each bit, each drink. Imagine the Spirit of God entering into you as you eat this orange, nourishing you, healing you, sustaining you, feeding you. Record your thoughts and reflections in your journal.

How was your encounter with the orange? Was it mystical, or ordinary? It is said that God works in mysterious ways, and perhaps sometimes the most extraordinary and mystical point is actually made in a very ordinary way, with very ordinary means. That could well be the case in this story of Moses and the Burning Bush, for although this story is often presented as a miraculous encounter with God in which God revealed God's self to Moses in an unnatural way, modern day scripture scholarship suggests that what Moses witnessed in the burning bush was a natural occurrence and that the miracle of the story is that Moses saw the magnificence of God in something completely ordinary. As you took part in the exercise with the orange, perhaps you got a glimpse into what Moses may have experienced.

As a younger man, Moses killed an Egyptian who was beating one of his fellow-Hebrews. Moses fled to the desert of Midian with the price of death on his head. In the desert, he made a life for himself and was able to escape prosecution. During this peaceful existence, Moses was able to deny the persecution that his people were suffering at the hands of the Egyptians. He was able to remain ignorant and blind to the slavery he had left behind. When Moses looked upon the burning bush and became aware of the wondrous nature of God, he was awakened out of his sleep and could no longer ignore the truth that urgently spoke within him. He knew that he could not remain in the freedom of Midian while his people suffered in bondage. Having had the personal experience of liberation, he knew firsthand what his people were missing. The burning bush woke him up out of his denial and ignited the spark within him of the truth that set him free and would eventually free the Hebrew people.

The revelation that Moses experienced in the burning bush is a revelation for us as well. God illuminates truth to us each and every day through the natural and ordinary world. The invitation is to be open to seeing the ordinary through extraordinary eyes. When we are open to seeing the world through God's eyes, the miraculous begins to appear. We realize that everything in our natural world is an expression of God's grace and an example of the freedom and joy that God intends for us. In seeing the world through God's eyes, we can truly see the "good and gracious land, flowing with milk and honey." To connect more fully with this revelation, we need only be open to seeing the world through the eyes of God.

SPIRITUAL VISION

In the thirteenth year, on the first day of the fourth month, while I was among the exiles by the river Chebar, the heavens opened, and I saw divine visions . . .

*As I looked, a storm wind came from the North, a huge
cloud with flashing fire, for the midst of which something
gleamed like electrum. Within it were figures resembling four
living creatures that looked like this: their form was human, but
each had four faces and four wings, and their legs went straight
down; the soles of their feet were round. The sparkled with a
gleam like burnished bronze . . .*

Such was the vision of the likeness of the glory of the Lord.

*When I had seen it, I feel upon my face and heard a voice
that said to me: Son of man, stand up! I wish to speak with
you . . . Son of man, I am sending you to the Israelites . . .*

Ezekiel 1:1, 4-7, 28b; 2:1, 3

While Moses had a vision of the extraordinary through his physical
vision, Ezekiel experienced a vision beyond the physical—what
could be referred to as *spiritual vision*. A spiritual vision is something
that we see during our waking hours that is seen, but not through
our physical eyes. Vision of this sort is seen through our creative
imagination and our daydreams, but is no less real than what we
see with our physical eyes. Creative visualization, daydreaming and
imagination are the vehicles through which this kind of vision is
made manifest.

Jean-Yves Leloup calls this vehicle of spiritual sight the *nous*.
"In the Gospel of Mary, the nous is not presented as the fully Divine
in us, but as the intermediary between the realm of psych (soul) and
the realm of Pneuma (Spirit). It is the Pneuma—the Breath, or Holy
Spirit—that is considered truly Divine in the anthropology of this
gospel. This brings us to a fourfold anthropology in which the nous
also finds its rightful place . . . Thus the human being is a composite
of body (soma), soul (psyche), mind (nous) and Spirit (Pneuma)"
(Gospel of Mary Magdalene pg. 120)

When Jean-Yves Leloup uses the word *mind* to describe spiritual sight, he is not talking about mind in the usual sense, as being connected with the intellect. Instead, he is referring to the place within us where we are able to connect with and receive God's truth. As he describes it, the *nous* is the intermediary between our fully human self and God. In this way, the *nous* transcends even spiritual sight to encompass all the ways in which God's truth is revealed to us, referring to the place within us where we are one with the mind of God.

Spiritual vision is another of those vehicles of revelation that is often ignored, discredited or even maligned. Because spiritual vision is typically singular in nature, meaning that the revelation is only witnessed by the receiver, it is impossible to prove through eye-witness accounts. Additionally, spiritual vision rarely leaves behind any physical evidence. As such, we have only the receiver's testimony upon which to base the case. Spiritual vision cannot be explained nor proven and requires a leap of faith and trust in order for belief to take place.

Neither affirmation of this gift nor effective tools for its cultivation are readily accessible. Without affirmation and proper support, the person who receives an experience of spiritual vision may initially think they are insane, or attribute the vision to some sort of visual disturbance. This lack of support creates a great obstacle to the receiver in their ability to give credit to their experience, embrace its gift and share it with others. The invitation is to be open to the possibility that spiritual vision can occur while seeking and practicing opportunities in which spiritual vision may be received.

Spiritual vision is typically received in one of two ways: spontaneously or intentionally. Spontaneous spiritual vision occurs when the mind of God breaks through our visual barriers and reveals a vision of truth. In these situations, we are usually going about our normal business when we suddenly see something unexpected that reveals truth in some way and is visible to no one but us. This seems to be the kind of vision witnessed by Ezekiel in the previous reading.

The second way in which spiritual vision can occur is through our "creative imagination,"—another way of saying "daydreaming with intention." Through this process, we engage our creative imagination with the intention of opening up to God's truth. God is then able to work through our daydreaming in the same way that God works through our dreams. St. Ignatius of Loyola was the first to give credit to this as an effective and valid form of prayer. While lying in the hospital, recovering from wounds received in battle, he took to daydreaming. First, he daydreamed about his future greatness; then he discovered a book on the life of Christ. He began reading the text and brought these words into his daydreams. A wealth of comfort, insight and inspiration was received by Ignatius through this process—a wealth that is waiting there for us as well.

Integration

You are invited to practice spiritual vision through an exercise of Imagination/Contemplation. Read through the following scripture passage, looking for a character that speaks to you. Go back and prayerfully read through the passage from the perspective of this character. Now enter into a period of creative imagination, allowing the story to unfold in your mind from the vantage point of your chosen character. Imagine every detail—the setting, the scenery, the other characters present, what you are wearing, the weather, etc. Allow your imagination run free as the story unfolds in your imagination. Allow God to speak to you through your imagination. Record your reflection in your journal, allowing additional details to emerge as you write. Go back and reflect on the feeling and the emotions that emerged and reflect on how God was speaking to you through the emerging details.

In the sixth month, the angel Gabriel was sent from God to a town of Galilee called Nazareth, to a virgin betrothed to a man named Joseph, of the house of David, and the virgin's name was Mary. And coming to her, he said, "Hail, favored one! The Lord is with you." But she was greatly troubled at what was said and pondered what sort of greeting this might be. Then the angel said to her, "Do not be afraid, Mary, for you have found favor with God. Behold, you will conceive in your womb and bear a son, and you shall name him Jesus. He will be great and will be called Son of the Most High, and the Lord God will give him the throne of David his father, and he will rule over the house of Jacob forever, and of his kingdom there will be no end." But Mary said to the angel, "How can this be, since I have no relations with a man?" And the angel said to her in reply, "The Holy Spirit will come upon you, and the power of the Most High will overshadow you. Therefore the child to be born will be called holy, the Son of God. And, behold, Elizabeth, your relative, has also conceived a son in her old age, and this is the sixth month for her who was called barren; for nothing will be impossible for God." Mary said, "Behold, I am the handmaid of the Lord. May it be done to me according to your word." Then the angel departed from her.

Luke 1:26-38

DREAMS

Hebrew and Christian scripture are filled with stories of men and women receiving insight, direction and truth from God through their dreams. Joseph (of Dreamcoat fame) from the book of Genesis and Joseph, the husband of Mary, are the two most notable receivers of truth through dreams. Unfortunately, we are tempted to believe that God could only speak through these holy people, and that our dreams are insignificant and merely a function of our restless minds. Fortunately, modern-day psychology has helped us to rediscover the importance and significance of dreams in revealing truth.

Modern psychology has shown us that dreams are a valuable tool for accessing the secrets of the unconscious mind. Dreams provide a vehicle through which the hidden truths within us may find their expression. In this way, dreams become a powerful means by which truth is revealed. Dreams are able to communicate truth in a way that pierces through the defense mechanisms and filters through which we often sensor our truth. By speaking in metaphor, dreams are able to communicate truth in a way that allows us to receive only what we are ready to receive at any given place in our journey. As such, dreams can be returned to again and again where deeper levels of meaning continue to be revealed. In the end, when we approach dreams with the intention of receiving the Divine truth hidden in the symbols, we will find that,

"Surely, interpretations (of dreams) come from God."
Genesis 40:8b

Opening up to dreams as communicators of God's truth allows us to reclaim the one third of our life spent in sleep as time spent in Oneness with God.

The number of ways in which we can approach dream interpretation is limitless and each school of psychological thought has its preferred technique. All techniques offer a key through which God's truth can be more fully revealed. Although there are those rare situations where dreams can be taken as literal truth, as was experienced by Joseph, husband of Mary, or prophetic as experienced through Joseph of Egypt, modern psychology's focus is on the dream as a metaphor—a symbol for something deeper. When approached from this perspective, we can allow our ego to step aside so that God's truth can be revealed through the images and emotions of our dreams.

> *Now this is how the birth of Jesus Christ came about. When his mother Mary was betrothed to Joseph, but before they lived together, she was found with child through the Holy Spirit. Joseph her husband, since he was a righteous man, yet unwilling to expose her to shame, decided to divorce her quietly. Such was his intention when, behold, the angel of the Lord appeared to him in a dream and said, "Joseph, son of David, do not be afraid to take Mary your wife into your home, For it is through the Holy Spirit that this child has been conceived in her. She will bear a son and you are to name him Jesus, because he will save his people from their sins." . . . When Joseph awoke, he did as the angel of the Lord had commanded him and took his wife into his home.*
>
> Matthew 1:18-21, 24

Integration

In this exercise, you will have an opportunity to open to God's truth being revealed in a dream. If you don't have a dream that is readily accessible, wait until you have a memorable dream to do this exercise. When you have a memorable dream, as soon as possible after waking, write down the dream as you remember it. Pay special attention to the emotions that you experienced during the dream and while recording it. After you have written the dream, go back and circle every noun (person, place or thing). On a separate sheet of paper, in one column, write down each noun. In a separate column, write a description of that noun—describe the noun as if you are describing it to an alien who has no previous experience with that object. Now go back to your narrative and replace each circled noun with the new description. Read the new narrative to yourself. You may be surprised to see what is revealed in this retelling.

INTUITION

Intuition is the small voice of God within us that interrupts our rational thoughts and leads us on the path of truth. Intuition is one of the many ways in which God reveals truth to us, and is an often overlooked and under-appreciated gift from God because intuition often flies in the face of reason and rational thought.

Intuition is often considered a "woman thing" as we bear witness to the innumerable times that women for no apparent reason know when their children are suffering, awake in the middle of the night just moments before their child begins to choke, knows who is on the phone before even picking up. Fortunately, this gift is not reserved solely for women and is in fact, available to everyone. Perhaps women have just been given greater permission to cultivate and honor this gift. It may have been intuition that guided Elizabeth to recognize the movement of the child in her womb as a message of truth from God:

> *During those days Mary set out and traveled to the hill country in haste to a town of Judah, where she entered the house of Zechariah and greeted Elizabeth. When Elizabeth heard Mary's greeting, the infant leaped in her womb, and Elizabeth, filled with the Holy Spirit, cried out in a loud voice and said, "Most blessed are you among women, and blessed is the fruit of*

*your womb. And how does it happen to me? For at the moment
the sound of your greeting reached my ears, the infant in my
womb leaped for joy. Blessed are you who believed that what
was spoken to you by the Lord would be fulfilled."*

Luke 1:39-45

As we allow ourselves to be open to the gift of intuition, we discover that God's truth is right here, at our fingertips, we need only be open to seeing and believing. Intuition serves as a compass that we can consult as we seek direction in our daily lives. Intuition allows us to depart from the world of the mind and rational thought to reside in the presence of God. Intuition invites us to trust our hearts, trust our guts and trust that tiny voice of truth that speaks within us. Each and every one of us has use of this gift and we grow in our ability to exercise this gift when we put it into practice. With intuition practice makes perfect. Through practice, we set aside our own egos and allow God to become our leader and guide. Trusting this guidance, we are free to enjoy what God intends for our highest good, no longer stranded in our illusionary world of wants and desires.

WISDOM

Intuition is a knowledge or awareness that comes out of a place of innocence. It is a pure awareness of truth based on no prior knowledge, experience or learning. Intuition has no rational explanation and seems to come literally from nowhere. As intuition reveals truth, we wonder, "Where did that come from?" Wisdom, on the other hand is an awareness based partly on previous experience, knowledge or expertise. Wisdom is rooted in our past experience and integrates this knowledge with Divine truth. God reveals truth in this way by activating our unique gifts for reasoning, discernment and applied knowledge and infuses it with God's truth. In this way, we are able to remain detached from our human expectations while harnessing our life experience so that truth may be revealed in a way that transcends our limited perceptions.

Perhaps it was wisdom that led Moses' mother and sister to place him in the papyrus basket and leave him among the reeds on the river bank (Exodus 1:22; 2:1-10). It does not seem that it was simply pure luck that placed the Pharaoh's daughter in a place where she would obviously take notice of the basket with the crying baby lying among the reeds. Miriam, Moses' sister must have had prior knowledge of this being the place where Pharaoh's daughter would bathe. Of course, there was no way of knowing that the Pharaoh's daughter would take pity on the child and take him as her own, but it would have been a risk worth taking. Fortunately, for Moses, the Pharaoh's daughter chose compassion. Then, in a moment of inspired wisdom, Miriam offered to find a woman to nurse the child and at least for the time of nursing, Moses was returned to his own mother. Wisdom, prior knowledge inspired by God's truth, moved Miriam and her mother to action on that day and out of their combined gift of wisdom, Moses was saved and they had the opportunity to play a significant role in his life. Under the fosterage of Pharaoh's daughter, Moses grew into manhood and enjoyed the privilege of the other princes of court, something he would never have been able too enjoy as a Hebrew slave.

Wisdom, it seems is the source and the goal of the knowledge of God. As it is said in scripture:

> *If you receive my words and treasure my commands,*
> *Turning your ear to wisdom, inclining your heart to under-*
> *standing;*
> *Yes, if you call to intelligence, and to understanding raise your*
> *voice;*
> *If you seek her like silver, and like hidden treasure seek her*
> *out:*

Then will you understand the awe of the Lord;
The knowledge of God you will find;
For the Lord gives wisdom,
From God's mouth come knowledge and understanding.

Proverbs 2:1-6

And the gift of wisdom is this:

He who obeys me (wisdom) dwells in security, in peace, without
fear of harm.

Proverbs 1:33

Through wisdom we are able to relinquish the so-called truth that our ego would want us to perceive and can see instead through the eyes of God where true contentment, peace and security dwell. We realize that by our own efforts, we know nothing and that the true source of knowledge is in God alone. From this place of humility we are able to surrender to the truth that God would reveal in God's time, all for our highest good. It then becomes the light of God that illuminates our way while, at the same time, illuminating the highest truth within.

HOLY VIRTUE—ZEAL

We are able to receive God's truth for us when we remember that *we are one with the mind of God.* Remembering this oneness allows us to be healed of the fear that *we do not or cannot know the truth.* Releasing this fear then allows us to refrain from the spiritual compulsion of *sloth* that deters us from seeking and discerning truth in our lives. As we freely and openly use these gifts that God gave us to reason, discern and exercise truth, we come to know the holy virtue of *zeal*. No longer deferring to external perceived authority, we are able to enthusiastically pursue the search for truth and even more enthusiastically work toward embracing and living out this truth. We are no longer caught in the trap of group think as we confidently stand in the truth that God has revealed to us directly. Seeking and embracing God's truth allows us to live the life of freedom that God intended. Then we shall be like the Psalmist who wrote:

"Zeal for your house consumes me."

Psalm 69:10

CHAPTER NINE

You Are One With God

Jesus prayed, "And I have given them the glory you gave me, so that they may be one, as we are one, I in them and you in me, that they may be brought to perfection as one, that the world may know that you sent me, and that you love them even as you loved me."

John 17:22-23

THE FEAR—I AM ALONE

Clinging to the myths we have been told and the dogma that we have been taught, we find ourselves caught in the endless loop of human suffering. Our life experiences further compound this suffering by enforcing this false perception of separation from God and from one another. Our mistaken perception that we are separate from God prevents us from experiencing the harmonious connection that we share with God and with all that God has dreamed into existence for us. When we cannot sense this connection, we fear the worst— that *we are alone.* This false sense of "aloneness" then shows up in our lives as the compulsion of *pride.*

DEADLY COMPULSION—PRIDE

There is an ancient saying that states, "Pride goeth before the fall." This sentiment could not be more true—but not in the way we usually think of it. Traditionally, this idea has been associated with the Genesis story of the fall of man, in which pride caused our disobedience, and the resulting disobedience caused our banishment from Paradise.

However, Authentic Freedom provides the opposite perspective from which to examine this "sin" of *pride*—not as the cause of our sense of separation, but rather, as the effect.

If we believe in God's gift of free will, we must also believe that we freely choose the human experience—the experience of ourselves as seemingly separate from God. This choice is freely given by our compassionate and loving God, not as a punishment, but as an opportunity to experience God more fully. Yet, despite knowing that we face consequences for choosing illusion, we choose it anyway for the sake of our own learning, growth and transformation. But God knows the suffering we experience in making this choice, and waits expectantly for our decision to turn away from this illusion and freely reclaim our birthright—our oneness with our God, in love. We have the opportunity to choose God over the human experience, illusion. Until we consciously make this choice, we feel rejected, alone and afraid. It is out of this fear that the deadly compulsion of *pride* emerges.

Pride is another word for ego. *Pride* is the consequence of our choice to falsely perceive ourselves as separate from God. Pride/ego is the part of our selves that falsely believes "I have to do it alone. I can do it alone. There is no God. I am all there is." *Pride* is the compulsion that emerges to protect the human experiment and make it appear real. If our true nature is Oneness with God, then *pride* or ego could also be thought of as our false self, and it is this false self that clings to the human experiment. Thriving on compulsion and fear, the ego fights to stay alive by preventing us from remembering the truth of who we are.

In a sense, the ego is necessary, for without it the human experiment would cease to exist. The ego must remain somewhat intact in order for us to continue being human. But at some point, attachment to the ego becomes the root of our human suffering, fear and compulsions. In fact, the *seven core fears* all have their origin in the *ego/pride*. If we want to experience less suffering, release our fears and be healed of our compulsions, we must do the work of shedding the ego so that we can reclaim the awareness of the love that we are.

Integration

Take some time to reflect on the presence of *pride* in your own life. It may help to answer the following questions:

- Where do you believe yourself to be separate from God?
- Where do you think you have to do it alone, that there is no Divine Source to assist you or lead you to assistance?
- Where do you believe you can do it alone?
- What is your experience of loneliness?
- Have you been in contact with the deep longing within that seeks to be filled?
- How have you responded to that longing?
- Have you sought fulfillment outside of yourself through activities, things, people, or have you recognized it as God calling to remember the love that you are?

EASTERN MEDICINE AS A TOOL FOR HEALING— THE CROWN CHAKRA

This alignment with God is something that we have the opportunity to feel spiritually, emotionally, mentally and physically. It is through the chakras that this alignment can be experienced and observed. The *crown chakra*, located at the top of our head, is the energy center through which we remember that we are One with God. When we are fully attuned to our connection with God, the *crown chakra* is balanced and open. When we have forgotten our intimate connection with God, the *crown chakra* reflects a state of imbalance and constriction. Because the *crown chakra* is the most spiritually oriented, the physical symptoms related to it are subtle. The symptoms of the *crown chakra* in a state of disharmony manifest themselves on the level of consciousness. Psychic paralysis, disorientation, dizziness, and disorders of the central nervous system, the cerebral cortex and the pituitary gland, could very well have their origins in an imbalanced crown chakra. If you are facing issues in any of these areas, it may be helpful to explore your perception of Oneness with God.

An imbalance in the *crown chakra* can be most acutely felt as a deep sense of loneliness, depression or despair. When we falsely believe ourselves as separate from God, we are left with a deep longing. This longing is God calling us home.

Integration

Take time to connect with the sensation of the *crown chakra*. Sit in silence as you imagine an opening at the crown of your head. From that opening, visualize a brilliant white light coming up out of your head and reaching towards the heavens. Imagine that light connecting you with the God of your understanding. Allow yourself to remember that this light is not only connecting you with God, but is the very Spirit of God that lives in and through you. Imagine that same kind of light emanating from the Divine Source and reaching into the crowns of all people on this earth. Visualize the connection between God, all of creation and yourself. Pay attention to any feelings, emotions, thoughts and reflections that may arise during this activity.

SACRED TRUTH—YOU ARE ONE WITH GOD AND THEREFORE, NEVER ALONE

> *Jesus prayed, "And I have given them the glory you gave me, so that they may be one, as we are one, I in them and you in me, that they may be brought to perfection as one, that the world may know that you sent me, and that you love them even as you loved me."*
>
> John 17:22-23

As we are reminded in John's gospel, Jesus had come to know and understand the truth that *we are not alienated or separate from God.* We are, in fact, One with this God who is the very Source of our existence. Jesus' greatest desire was that we would grow to remember and fully believe in this Oneness. He knew that remembering this Oneness was the path to peace and the end of human suffering.

It is the false sense of separation from God that is the cause of all human suffering. Believing ourselves as separate, alienated or banished from God creates a deep longing within us and a profound sense of loneliness. This fear of separation is then lived out through the deadly compulsion of *pride*—believing we have to do it alone or conversely, believing that we can. This sense of separation manifests in an imbalance in the *crown chakra* and organs and functions to which its energy flows. Healing this false perception of separation is the ultimate intention and goal of the human journey. It is in remembering the truth of Oneness that peace and harmony may be restored and spiritual *humility* realized.

HOLY VIRTUE—HUMILITY

Humility is the understanding that without our Divine Source we are nothing. It is an attitude not of submission, but of recognition that in order to experience the fullness of our truth and the fulfillment of the way in which God desires to express God's self through us, we must turn to God for assistance. Alone, we cannot realize the truth of who we are, nor can we know contentment. When we are *humble*, we are open to allowing the Divine Source to live in and through us, setting aside our own fears and ego attachments to make room for the life the Divine intended to create through us.

When we allow ourselves to set aside our prideful perceptions and work toward remembering the truth that *we are One in God*, we experience the virtue of *humility*. We allow ourselves to be open to receiving God's highest good and accept it willingly. In accepting this path, we are exercising the spiritual quality of obedience. Obedience in the spiritual sense is not to be confused with our human experience of obedience which implies, "Do it because I told you." In Paul's letter to the Hebrews, we get a glimpse into how we might begin to understand this spiritual attitude of obedience.

> *Son though he was, he learned obedience from what he suffered; and when he was made perfect, he became the source of eternal salvation for all who obey him, declared by God high priest according to the order of Melchizedek.*
>
> Hebrews 5:8–10

Embracing this attitude of spiritual obedience, we turn to God for guidance, direction, knowledge and truth and freely choose the path that God has revealed to be in our highest good. No longer operating out of our own ego, or out of the ego of another, we take a risk that what we discern to be from God is indeed from God, and we trust in this path. Living this kind of obedience requires the most profound leap of faith, the results of which prove to be far beyond what we could ever have imagined or created for ourselves.

When we are able to trust in this way, we shall know the peace and freedom of living in the grace of God.

Afterword

Whenever a person turns to the Lord the veil is removed. Now the Lord is the Spirit and where the Spirit of the Lord is, there is freedom.

2 Corinthians 16-17

Now we come full circle in the journey toward embracing a life of authentic freedom. The *core wound*—the false perception of separation from God—is the origin of the *seven core fears* and their resulting compulsions—*gluttony, lust, wrath, envy, greed, sloth* and *pride*. It is through the awareness of the chakra system that we begin to recognize these compulsions in action. Through the *seven sacred truths*, we are able to heal the seven fears and their corresponding compulsions and work toward embracing the *seven cardinal virtues* of *temperance, fortitude, mercy, compassion, generosity, zeal* and *humility*. Living these virtues, we find the false perception of separation from God and from one another (the core wound) falling away. Healing this *core wound* is the ultimate goal and destination of our human journey and leads us into the spiritual freedom that God intended.

Freedom, understood from a spiritual perspective, is God's deepest desire for us and God's loving hand has planted the desire in our hearts to return to this state of freedom. This Divine desire compels, urges, provokes, inspires and guides (and nags, goads, tortures, taunts) us along the path to its realization. This divinely ordained freedom, known by its deep state of peace, joy and love, has nothing to do with our external circumstances, as it is, by its very nature, an internal quality. Divine freedom is expansive, life-giving and filled with growth and promise. When we are able to name and claim the truth that God reveals to us as our highest good, we enjoy the greatest expression of spiritual freedom. The process of authentic freedom provides the tools through which this freedom can be embraced and enjoyed. This journey, however, would not be complete without one critical tool for spiritual growth: *discernment*.

DISCERNMENT

Discernment is the informal or formal process through which we distinguish the voice of God from the voice of the false self or ego. The voice of God leads us toward freedom. The ego, on the other hand, is the voice of temptation trying to keep us from our Divinely ordained path. The ego, like the devil sitting on our shoulder, whispers guilt, fear, worry, wants and desires into our ears, tempting us away from the path of God. In contrast, God's voice is like the angel sitting on the opposite shoulder, inviting us to choose the path that is in our highest good. Discernment allows us to freely choose the path that will be uniquely in our highest good. The good news is that God makes the knowledge of this path available to all of us—if we only ask. This is what Jesus meant when he said,

> *"And I tell you, ask and you will receive; seek and you will find; knock and the door will be opened to you. For everyone who asks, receives; and the one who seeks, finds; and to the one who knocks, the door will be opened."*
>
> Luke 11:9-10

This scripture passage is not about getting what we want, but allowing each of us to be open to receiving what God knows is in our highest good, even if that differs from what we want for ourselves. This is the true path of humility and the meaning of the prayer,

"Your kingdom come, your will be done, on earth as it is in heaven."

Matthew 6:9b

Meditation and prayer are the vehicles through which we enter into this process of discernment, as are observation and support through our Spiritual Director, Counselor or close spiritual friends. Discernment allows us to hear the voice of God more clearly and to recognize the voice of the ego which strives to imprison us in the status quo. While this can be a confusing and challenging process, scripture provides some valuable support:

Whenever a person turns to the Lord the veil is removed. Now the Lord is the Spirit and where the Spirit of the Lord is, there is freedom.

2 Corinthians 16-17

As Paul reveals, the ultimate test in the process of discernment is freedom—Does this path or choice give me peace, allow me to know love more fully, experience contentment and joy; is it expansive, life-giving and supportive?" If the answer to these questions is yes, then perhaps the path is being revealed to be "of God." If the answer is no, then perhaps what we have discerned is coming out of our fears, false perceptions, and ego attachments. Responding to the voice of God and stepping into the ever-expanding path of freedom, we are able to live more fully within the peace and compassion that is our original nature, while releasing the fears and ego attachments that hold us back.

Entering into the process of authentic freedom with the support of sound discernment, the foundation is established upon which Divine freedom can take root and grow. As we grow spiritually and allow ourselves to be healed of our inner wounds, this is a process that can be returned of again and again in your desire to remember your true nature while embracing a profound and lasting peace.

Appendix A

ABUNDANCE

FEAR	There is not enough.
COMPULSION	Gluttony
SACRED TRUTH	Your Divine Source meets all of your needs in abundance.
CHAKRA	Root

How We Experience This Fear Being Indulged

EMOTIONS	Fear, insecurity, restlessness, ungroundedness.
BEHAVIORS	Compulsive spending, buying, collecting, consumerism, wastefulness, self-deprivation, over and under eating.
PHYSICAL	Weight problems (too much, too little), eating disorders, leg, knees, feet problems, constipation, hemorrhoids, sciatica, difficulty bringing ideas, dreams, visions into reality. Adrenal disorders. Problems with teeth, bones, large intestines, colon.
ELEMENT	Earth

Evidence of Healing

INNER STATE	Stillness, security, stability, faith and trust, ability to bring dreams into reality.
VIRTUE	Temperance
GRACE	Peace

YOU ARE UNIQUELY GIFTED

FEAR	I will be unable to bring forth life that will persist.
COMPULSION	Lust
SACRED TRUTH	You are co-creator with God and when you surrender to this process, together you bring forth life that persist.
CHAKRA	Sacral

How We Experience This Fear Being Indulged

EMOTIONS	Desperation, powerlessness.
BEHAVIORS	Abuse of power or being abused by power, addictions, co-dependency, lack of boundaries, unhealthy sexual behaviors and compulsions, not expressing the life within us.
PHYSICAL	Impotence, frigidity, uterine, bladder or kidney trouble, stiff lower back, reproductive organ issues, prostate cancer, uterine, ovarian, cervical cancers.
ELEMENT	Water

Evidence of Healing

INNER STATE	Balanced emotions, ability to "let go", healthy intimate relationships, creativity.
VIRTUE	Fortitude
GRACE	Contentment

YOU CAN DO IT!

FEAR	I can't.
COMPULSION	Wrath
SACRED TRUTH	There is nothing outside of you that can keep you from living freely as your most authentic self—the person God has made you to be.
CHAKRA	Solar Plexus

How We Experience This Fear Being Indulged

EMOTIONS	Anger, rage, resentment, paralysis, impatience, irritability.
BEHAVIORS	Projecting, lashing out, building resentments, unhealthy expressions of anger, depression (anger turned inward), worry.
PHYSICAL	Ulcers, diabetes, hypoglycemia, digestive disorders, liver and gallbladder issues, immune system disorders, pancreas, spleen.
ELEMENT	Fire

Evidence of Healing

INNER STATE	Laughter, joy, self-esteem, willpower, forgiveness.
VIRTUE	Mercy
GRACE	Empowerment

YOU ARE LOVED!

FEAR	I am not loved.
COMPULSION	Envy
SACRED TRUTH	God is love and you are made of this love. This love cannot be denied, nor does it need to be earned—it is your very being.
CHAKRA	Heart

How We Experience This Fear Being Indulged

EMOTIONS	Grief, sadness, despondency.
BEHAVIORS	Withdrawing, difficulty trusting, lack of compassion or empathy, anger and resentment (used as a self-defense mechanism), victim behavior (poor me!).
PHYSICAL	Heart or lung problems, high blood pressure, asthma, problems in the arms or hands, immune system (thymus).
ELEMENT	Air

Evidence of Healing

INNER STATE	Love, compassion, joy, mercy.
VIRTUE	Mercy
GRACE	Joy

YOUR TRUTH SHALL SET YOU FREE

FEAR	I am not free to express my truth.
COMPULSION	Greed
SACRED TRUTH	Expressing your truth shall set you free.

How We Experience This Fear Being Indulged

EMOTIONS	Restlessness, anger, anxiety, irritability, feeling of being insane or out of control.
BEHAVIORS	Panic or anxiety attacks, withdrawal, depression, repression, problems communicating, expressing your needs.
PHYSICAL	Problems of the neck, shoulders, upper back, throat, mouth, teeth, thyroid, fibromyalgia.
ELEMENT	Sound

Evidence of Healing

INNER STATE	Cohesive movement of ideas into reality.
VIRTUE	Generosity
GRACE	Freedom

YOU DO KNOW

FEAR	I do not know.
COMPULSION	Sloth
SACRED TRUTH	All wisdom, knowledge and truth are available to you through God.
CHAKRA	Brow

How We Experience This Fear Being Indulged

EMOTIONS	Confusion, laziness, lack of motivation, not wanting to accept responsibility.
BEHAVIOR	Deferring to "perceived" authority rather than taking responsibility for discerning our own truth. Lack of faith/belief. Ignorance, prejudice, racism, discrimination, legalistic behavior, rigidity, believing you (or someone else) have the absolute truth. Believing that there is such a thing as absolute truth.
PHYSICAL	Headaches, eye issues, dizziness.
ELEMENT	Light

Evidence of Healing

INNER STATE	Openness to seeing and believing the truth as it is revealed to you, and taking responsibility for it.
VIRTUE	Zeal
GRACE	Knowledge, Understanding

YOU ARE ONE WITH GOD

FEAR	I am alone.
COMPULSION	Pride
SACRED TRUTH	You are one with God and therefore, never alone.
CHAKRA	Crown

How We Experience This Fear Being Indulged

EMOTIONS	Depression, alienation, confusion, boredom, apathy.
BEHAVIOR	Arrogance, operating out of our ego, believing we can or have to do it alone.
PHYSICAL	Confusion, physical heaviness, feeling of being paralyzed, pituitary gland issues, cerebral cortex, central nervous disorders.
ELEMENT	Consciousness

Evidence of Healing

INNER STATE	Detachment, cooperation, knowing and living in oneness with God and all of creation. Seeking and surrendering to Divine Guidance.
VIRTUE	Humility
GRACE	Bliss/Wisdom

Appendix B

YOUR ENERGY ANATOMY

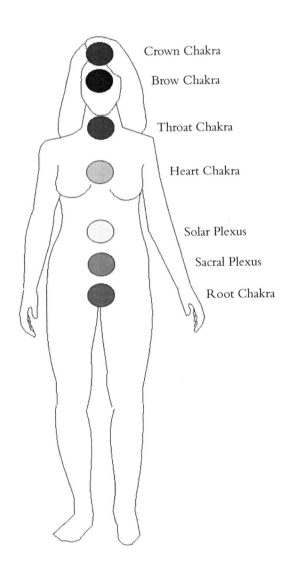

Crown Chakra

Brow Chakra

Throat Chakra

Heart Chakra

Solar Plexus

Sacral Plexus

Root Chakra

Suggested Reading

Douglas-Klotz, Neil, *The Hidden Gospel: Decoding the Spiritual Message of the Aramaic Jesus*, Quest Books, Wheaton, 1999.

Douglas-Klotz, Neil, *Prayers of the Cosmos*, Harper One, San Francisco, 1993.

Ericco, Rocco A. *Setting a Trap for God: The Aramaic Prayer of Jesus*, Unity Books, Unity Village, 1997.

Judith, Anodea, *Wheels of Life: A User's Guide to the Chakra System*, Llewellyn Publications, St. Paul, 1987.

Kubler-Ross, Elizabeth, *On Death and Dying*, Scribner Classics, New York, 1997.

Leloup, Jean-Yves, *The Gospel of Mary Magdalene*, Inner Traditions, Rochester, 2002.

Leloup, Jean-Yves, *The Gospel of Thomas*, Inner Traditions, Rochester, 2005.

Levine, Peter A., *Waking the Tiger: Healing Trauma*, North Atlantic Books, Berkeley, 1997.

Mirdad, Michael, *The Seven Initiations of the Spiritual Path*, A.R.E. Press, Virginia Beach, 2004.

Myss, Caroline, *Anatomy of the Spirit: The Seven Stages of Power and Healing*, Three Rivers Press, New York, 1997.

Ramsay, Jay, *The Crucible of Love: The Path to Passionate and True Relationships*, O Books, 2005.

Schwan, Marie, Syrup-Bergin, Jacqueline, *Love: A Guide for Prayer*, St. Mary's Press, Winona, 1985.

Senior, Donald, Editor, *The Catholic Study Bible* (translation of the New American Bible); Oxford University Press, New York, 1990.

Servan-Schreiber, M.D., PhD, David, *The Instinct to Heal: Curing Depression, Anxiety and Stress without Drugs and without Talk Therapy*, Rodale Books, Emmaus, 2004.

Index

Ego Attachment, 48, 65, 159, 163
Eli, 111–113
Elizabeth (Mother of John the
    Baptist), 76 (Luke), 114, 144
    (Luke), 147–148 (Luke)
Energy, 4
    Anatomy, 173
    Balance/Imbalance, 4
    Brow Chakra, 132
    Center, 105, 132, 156–157
    Chakra, 5, 72, 75, 86, 89
    Creative, 55–56, 67, 69
    Crown Chakra, 156
    Divine, 4, 55
    Eastern Culture, 4
    Flow, 3, 39, 56, 133, 158
    God Within Us, 47–48, 55–57
    Heart Chakra, 85
    Inner Gifts, 55
    Love, 72, 75, 86, 89
    Money, 69
    Physical Correspondences, 51
    Procreation, 47–48, 54
    Reiki, 5
    Root Chakra, 7, 39
    Sacral Chakra, 53
    Solar Plexus, 72, 75, 86, 89
    System, 132
    "The Power" by Amy Grant,
        67
    Throat Chakra, 105
Envy, 10, 83–84, 89, 161, 168

F
Fall of Man, 83, 154
    See also *Adam and Eve; Garden
        of Eden*

Fire, 72–74, 91, 113, 138 (Exodus),
    141 (Ezekiel), 144, 167
Forgive, 94
Forgiven, 26, 38 (Luke)
Forgiveness, 19, 79, 94, 167
Forgiving, 94
Fortitude, 10, 60, 161, 166
Free Will, 154
Freedom, 1–2, 9, 14, 44, 54, 65–66,
    71, 103, 107, 111, 113, 131, 140,
    151, 159, 161–164

G
Garden of Eden, 16, 83
    See also *Adam and Eve; Fall of Man*
Generosity, 10, 123, 161, 169
    Holy Virtue, 122
Gluttony, 10, 32–35, 39, 161, 165
God
    And Reiki, 4
    Perception of Separation, 17, 19,
        39, 42, 56, 66, 74, 82, 89, 95,
        108, 110, 125, 136, 153–154,
        157
    Punitive, 41–42, 83
    See also *Divine Source, Kingdom
        of God, Oneness, Sin*
Gospel of Mary Magdalene, 19, 26
Gospel of Philip, 26–27
Gospel of Thomas, 21, 23, 26–27,
    175
Grant, Amy, "The Power", 67
Greed, 10, 101, 103–104, 108, 161,
    169
    As Deadly Compulsion, 101
Grief, 60, 68–69, 87, 168
    See also *Anger*